DEAD

IN THE

PARK

DEAD
IN THE
PARK

The Frank May Chronicles

Lawrence Friedman

A QP Mystery

QP BOOKS
New Orleans, Louisiana

DEAD IN THE PARK
The Frank May Chronicles

A QP Mystery, published in 2015 by QP Books, an imprint of Quid Pro Books. An earlier version of this title was previously published in 2011 by iUniversity (Bloomington, Indiana) under the pseudonym Lawrence Mayer.

QUID PRO, LLC
5860 Citrus Blvd., Suite D-101
New Orleans, Louisiana 70123
www.qpbooks.com

ISBN 978-1-61027-316-9 (paperback)
ISBN 978-1-61027-318-3 (eBook)

Publisher's Cataloging-in-Publication

Friedman, Lawrence.
     Dead in the Park / Lawrence Friedman.
        p. cm.
     Series: *The Frank May Chronicles* (#1)
     ISBN 978-1-61027-316-9 (pbk.)
1. Lawyers—California—Fiction. 2. San Mateo (Cal.)—Fiction. 3. May, Frank (Fictitious character)—Fiction. I. Friedman, Lawrence. II. Title. III. Series.
PS357.F739 2015   813.'1'7851—dc22
                                             2015166932
                                                 CIP

for Leah, Jane, Amy, Sarah,
David, Lucy, and Irene

DEAD

IN THE

PARK

1

It all started with my client, Cynthia Greenhouse, and a dead body, lying in a park in Palo Alto, California. An unidentified dead body. Unidentified—and very mysterious. Yet this dead body was somehow connected to my client, Cynthia, which is how I got involved. Mind you, I didn't *want* to get involved; but life can play tricks on you.

An unidentified dead body. No wallet. No driver's license. Nothing to show who the body belonged to. Except one thing: a small piece of paper, sewed into an inside pocket of the dead man's jacket. That was what started the whole process going. You see, Cynthia's address and phone number were on that piece of paper.

But who on earth was this man? And who killed him, and why? And in what way was he connected to my client, Cynthia?

First, though, before we get on with the story, let me introduce myself. My name is Frank May. I'm forty-four years old, and I'm a lawyer, a member of the California bar, engaged in the private practice of law. I have my own small office, in San Mateo, California. San Mateo is a suburb, to the south of San Francisco. Maybe you're not familiar with the Bay Area. San Francisco lies at the tip of a peninsula. The city sticks out like a big thumb into the space between the ocean and San Francisco Bay. Where the two bodies of water meet, that's the famous Golden Gate, spanned by a wonderful bridge, the Golden Gate Bridge. The city of San Francisco is beautiful and famous. Tourists love it. They come from Bloomington, Indiana, from Wichita, Kansas; or from Asia, Europe, everywhere. They all love San Francisco. They ride on the cable cars. They go to Fisherman's Wharf. They explore the streets of Chinatown. They climb up and down the hills.

Personally, I think the city is overrated. I have to admit, though, that some of the views are terrific: mountains, the Marin headlands, the ocean, Alcatraz, Angel Island.

San Mateo is neither beautiful nor famous. No tourist has ever gone there. Still, it's my home base; it's where I do my work.

My practice is fairly ordinary: I have clients who need wills, or trusts, or powers of attorney. Some of them even die, which is unfortunate for them and their families, but not for me. Frankly, I make money when clients die. I'm not ashamed of that. I perform a service. I also handle the affairs of small businesses—a restaurant owner here and there, a guy who owns two car-wash establishments—that sort of thing. I get a free meal now and then from a client, and I'm entitled to a car wash, whenever I want one. It's a quality car wash, as far as I can tell. The free meal is usually a lot less exciting, except for desserts. None of my restaurant clients are listed in Zagat's.

I have good clients and some not so good ones. The good ones need legal work, pay promptly, and never make trouble for me. The not so good ones also need legal work, but they pay slowly and poorly; and some of them are, frankly, a pain in the neck. In the end, I do make a living. I think I'm a decent lawyer. I have high ethical standards, too. That's not unusual, I think, even though lawyers generally have a miserable reputation. They rank just above car salesmen, and far below dentists, in the scale of public esteem.

I have nothing to do with criminal law. I want to make that clear. Criminal law is for specialists. The rest of us won't touch it. I never even liked the subject when I went to law school. Criminal law got me one of my lowest grades. The professor, whose name was Sunderbock, was the very epitome of dullness. He was able to make murder, rape, and assorted crimes as dull as, say, mortgages and insurance policies. But I can't blame my aversion on Sunderbock. The fact is, I've been a nerd all my life. I wear glasses (not contacts). I'm very ordinary. I do my job, and I want nothing to do with criminal justice. My friend, Nolan Thom, he's in the criminal business. As a lawyer, I mean. His clients are as rotten a collection of scum as you would want to see. Mostly rich scum (the poor ones have to use public defenders), but scum nonetheless. Some of them, I imagine, are actually dangerous. If I try to do something for a client, and I don't succeed, I might lose the client, and I might also lose money. But nobody is going to shoot off my kneecaps. I like my kneecaps just the way they are.

Anyway, I hate the sight of blood. Not that Nolan sees much blood. But he enjoys his legal niche. He relishes crime and punishment. It turns him on, I suppose. I'm the opposite.

Still, life has a way of playing tricks on people, as I said. I don't pursue criminal law, but criminal law has a habit of pursuing me. An astonishing number of my clients have gotten involved, somehow, in murder and other sordid affairs. Either they're victims, or they're accused of killing somebody, or in some way they get tangled up in crime. And when this happens, they have a tendency to drag me into it, kicking and screaming as it were.

Death is no stranger to me, of course. As I told you, I handle wills, trusts, and estates of the dead. But what I expect, and what I usually get, is somebody dying a nice, clean, natural death. In a hospital or a hospice, whatever. Oh yes, there's an occasional accidental death. But not violent death. And yet: is it my karma or something I did in a prior life? I can't avoid murder, somehow. It runs after me. It's my nemesis.

To tell the truth, I sometimes get caught up in a criminal affair. I don't *want* to be involved, but when I *am* involved, sometimes the adrenalin starts to flow. Or, at the very least, my inveterate curiosity. Once in a great while, in my fantasy life, I like to think of myself as a kind of detective, like Hercule Poirot or Perry Mason, the great detectives of fiction. And, to be honest, in a couple of instances, I even succeeded in solving a case. Mostly through luck or blind chance. My little gray cells are OK for drafting wills, but less reliable when it comes to crime.

This story is about one of those chance situations. By accident, I became involved in a pretty sordid affair. It all began in my office, as I was speaking to my client, Cynthia Greenhouse. Cynthia was a woman of about forty, intelligent and attractive. She had some kind of position in marketing, at a hi-tech firm in Silicon Valley. She had been my client for a number of years. Not that she had much legal business, but I did help her out from time to time. One matter involved the estate of a relative. I also handled her divorce.

I don't normally do divorces. I'm superstitious about divorce. I've been married for twenty years to Celia, and we're doing just fine, thank you. Sometimes it seems as if every Tom, Dick and Harry gets a divorce. And every Jane, Jill, and Jessica. Not to mention Luke and Tiffany. We have no-fault divorce here in California. It's easier to get a divorce than to get a driver's license or a hunting license—or so it seems to me. After all, you *can* flunk the driver's test, and some people do; but if you ask for a divorce, for whatever reason, you get it.

I don't understand divorce. Our next door neighbors seemed like such nice people, and so much in love, with two cute children, a big shaggy dog, and a garden of killer hydrangeas. They got divorced, and it turned out he fooled around, and she had a drinking problem. I lost some of my faith in humanity. These were *neighbors*, people who smiled at us, friendly, quiet people who had us over for coffee; people, moreover, who put empty coke bottles in the proper bin, and dutifully flattened cardboard for recycling, and who went to city council meetings, and whose hedges were always, always trimmed.

It's a positive epidemic, divorce. I ask myself, why can't people get along? Of course I know the answer. It's very hard to get along. It's the hardest thing to do. Everybody seems to be looking out for number one. Number two just doesn't figure. Or else they find a new number two, who seems so much better than the old number two. Or sexier, maybe. But I'm hardly an expert on the subject.

Cynthia's divorce—all I knew was her side of the story, of course. Who knows what the real story was. She had been married to a man named Edgar Greenhouse. Edgar was a lawyer, like me. He in fact did do divorces. That was his main stock in trade. He was a family law specialist. Family law means (mostly) divorce, with a few custody cases thrown in, and even those are byproducts of divorce. It's really family-breakup-law. Anyway, maybe all these unhappy, quarreling, irrational couples drove him to drink. *Something* drove him to drink. I hope it wasn't Cynthia, but you never know. She seemed very normal to me, but for all I know, she might have had some serious perversions. I'm going to assume that's not true.

I'm spending a little time on Edgar, because, as you will see, he has an important role in this story, though not a happy one. Anyway, as I said, Edgar drank. He was also a serious depressive. Cynthia said to me, "Do you know what it's like, living with somebody who's clinically depressed? Believe me, Frank, it's a living hell."

"Was he always depressed?" I asked her.

"I think so. But you know, when you get married, you think, oh, that's all in the past. You know, you're totally in love, and you think, things will be different. Everything will be fine, because now he has me to take care of him; and I've got him, and life will be great. But then there was all that drinking...."

The drinking and the depression, after a while, were just too much for Cynthia to take. And Edgar, in the midst of some horrific argument, actually punched her. That was the end, as far as she was concerned.

"Just once," she said. "But once was enough. Oh, afterwards, he turned cold sober, and he was, like, I'm so sorry, I don't know what came over me, and I love you, and he started blubbering, and it won't happen again, and all of that. But it was like an epiphany for me. Frank, from that moment on, it was over. Finished. Enough. I had had enough. I wanted out. That's all there was to it."

It wasn't a difficult divorce. Edgar was a divorce and family lawyer, as I said. That could have meant complications, but he was as docile as a puppy dog. Whatever she wanted, that was okay with him. Money, whatever. Maybe he was too depressed to care. It was hard to tell.

There wasn't much money. In fact, Edgar was in debt. The

main asset was a house in Redwood City, California.

They had no children. So that complication was avoided.

At the time, I remember, she came to my office and spent half an hour crying. Not that she missed Edgar. She was glad to get rid of him. But divorce is always a blow. No, she had no regrets. "It's just ... well, it's all just so awful. You can't help feeling, you're a failure. Either you picked the wrong man, which I certainly did, or.... Well, in either case, it's a failure. If only he could have snapped out of it ... the liquor ... the depression...."

"They have drugs now, don't they? For depression."

"Edgar wouldn't take them."

Cynthia has a good job, and she's fairly well off. She sold the house in Redwood City for some absurd amount. This is California. We have perpetual housing bubbles. Every once in a while the bubble bursts, which in fact has happened. But before the bubble bursts, the housing market can be totally insane. The prices reach astronomical heights. I've had clients who moved from other places—one client had been living in Ithaca, New York, in a beautiful house, four bedrooms, two acres of land, he moved to the Bay Area and the shock nearly killed him. He told me what he got for his Ithaca house, a few hundred thousand dollars. He was happy to get that much. In the Bay Area, he was looking for a house. He asked me, "What could I get for that money, say, in Palo Alto? Or San Mateo?"

I said: "a mobile home? A parking space?"

Cynthia, however, had cashed in at the frothiest, bubbliest part of the market. She invested the money, and moved in with her married sister, Daisy, and her brother-in-law, Clyde Winters. Daisy and Clyde owned a big, rambling house in Palo Alto; six bedrooms, five baths, two stories, and a crushing mortgage. The house was a major extravagance, and they were only too happy to let Cynthia share the costs "Besides," as Cynthia put it, "My sister and I are very close."

Daisy and Clyde have one child, a three-year-old boy, little Clyde Junior. Clyde Junior is an adopted child. "There's just the two of us, Daisy and me, in our family," Cynthia said. "Our poor mother had just about given up hope of grandchildren. Here I am divorced, and no immediate prospects; and poor Daisy... they just weren't able to have children. She wanted children desperately, it was driving her crazy. I don't know what the problem was. They went to all sorts of doctors. I never asked. It's not the sort of thing you ask people. I mean, even a sister. And she never told me. Daisy—she's fairly private, close-mouthed, I mean, I used to tell her everything, like about my dates, when we were in high school, you know, who took me out, and what they did, or what they tried to do. I even told her when and how I lost my virginity, but she never reciprocated. Anyway, with her it's don't ask, don't tell.... They've got this kid now, and they're absolutely crazy about him, stark raving mad. Little Clyde, or Junior; I like to call him Junior."

Clyde Jr. was a beautiful child. I've seen him. They adopted him when he was a tiny infant. I didn't know who the birth parents were, and I never asked. Perhaps Daisy and Clyde would find this question awkward. It was Edgar Greenhouse who arranged the adoption, shortly before his marriage with Cynthia broke up.

Clyde's father, Mose, who's 83, also lives in the house. I had met Mose, even done some work for him. An amazing, feisty old man. His name was really Thutmose, which is ridiculous. His parents were amateur archaeologists, and were totally enamored of ancient Egypt. It's not that rare an obsession. People love mummies, for example. In museums, there's always a crowd around those exhibits, gawking at the mummies. Anyway, the Winters named their son Thutmose, and his sister (long since dead) Nefertiti. Everybody called him Mose. They called her Teetee.

There was another brother, Zack Winters, and he also figures in this story. But more of that later. I often wondered how he got away with a name like Zachary, which isn't Egyptian at all. Turns out it was his middle name. His actual first name was Anubis, but (no surprise), he preferred his middle name. Everybody called him Zack. He was in his 80's, maybe 86 or 87, and he lived in Mountain View.

Cynthia liked old Mose, Daisy's father-in-law. "He's a real character, but it's fun to have him around the house.... I like the idea of family," Cynthia said, "the house, it's like a commune. Our own mother, she lived in Arizona, and she passed away a while ago. Anyway, we didn't see her that often." Mose was a widower. Clyde's mother, Doris, was dead. Clyde had a twin brother, Claude. They were not identical twins, I hasten to add. In actual fact, they hardly even looked alike, and in personality they were very different. So this is not one of those stories where there are identical twins, and the whole thing hinges on the fact that you can't tell them apart. Anybody who wasn't blind could tell Claude and Clyde apart.

But if you had asked me, which nobody did, I would have said it was a mistake to name them Clyde and Claude. It should have been Clyde and Harry or Clyde and Joe. Clyde and Claude was too cutesy.

I think you need something more than a vowel to separate twins. Not that I'm an expert on twins. There are none in my family.

Claude was single, and lived in an apartment in Menlo Park, California. There was also a sister, whose name I can't remember. She lives in Boca Raton, Florida, and has no connection with this story. Her husband is an insurance broker. I met him once and found him intolerable. But, as I said, he's not at issue here.

The day Cynthia came to see me, and told me the story that let loose a whole chain of events, she was—no surprise— terrifically agitated. When she first called me on the phone, I could tell that something was wrong. I mean, *anybody* could have told. She sounded so upset, her voice had a kind of tremor, and at first I could hardly tell it was her.

"Frank, the most awful thing has happened. It's like something out of a nightmare. Honest to God.... I've got to see you."

"Sure, Cynthia. What is it?"

"I don't want to talk over the phone. Frank, I need advice, I need it badly."

I told her to come in as soon as she could. I had no appointments that afternoon. I was drafting a will, doing some paper-work, and doing research about custody disputes. Nothing that couldn't wait.

Half an hour later, she appeared at my office. Her eyes were red with tears. Her dyed blonde hair was in some disarray.

I handed her a Kleenex.

She told me what was, indeed, a strange story. As I mentioned, it concerned a dead body. The body had been found, in Lytton Park, a small park in downtown Palo Alto, not far from University Avenue, which is more or less the main street of Palo Alto. The park is only about one block square, and it's surrounded by houses, but at night it's very dark and nobody goes there. The body had been shoved into some bushes. An early morning jogger found the body, and called the police on his cell phone. The dead person was male, Caucasian, about 30 or 40 years old. He had been murdered—shot through the heart. The police searched the park, but found no signs of the murder weapon.

"Now here's the strange thing, Frank," she said. "This man.... he had no identification. No wallet, no papers, nothing, no drivers' license, keys, nothing at all.... He was wearing a jacket, though; it had pockets, but the pockets were empty. The police, however, later on found something—inside the lining of the jacket, sewed in, a little piece of paper. And on this piece of paper was written an address and phone number. Nothing else. Frank: now here's the horrible part—it was *our* address and phone number...."

"My God, Cynthia; that's awful. Who *was* this man?"

"Frank, I have no idea. You can imagine how we felt. The police came to the house, I was getting ready to go to work, we were having breakfast, you know, it was all so *normal* one minute, and then a minute later, I mean, your world turns upside down. I said: Daisy, the police are at the door. We couldn't imagine why on earth they would come. It's scary, believe me. A policeman came, and another man, a detective I think, and they started asking questions, and we said what is this all about ... and then, when they told us, well, I wanted to sink through the floor. They had a photograph, this dead man's face, none of us recognized it, but they said, when can you come down to the morgue and see if you have any idea who he is."

"That's so terrible, Cynthia."

"Anyway, we all had to go—well, not Clyde's father, they spared us that at least—but all the rest of us, we went to this dreadful place, the morgue, and we had to take a look at the dead body. Frank, I've never *seen* a dead body. Believe me, I don't want to ever see one again."

"And you really didn't recognize this man?"

"No. Absolutely not. His face was all awful, you know, I think dead people look that way. But he was a stranger. I would swear to that. A total stranger."

"So you have no idea who he was? No guesses?"

"Didn't you hear me, Frank? No idea. None."

"And no idea why he had your address, your phone number."

"Not the tiniest clue, Frank. We told that, to those police people. Of course, they don't believe us. They think we're lying. They asked so many questions.... I imagine they were trying to trip us up, the way they do on television. But they couldn't get anything out of us, for the simple reason that we didn't know anything. I swear it. I have no idea who he is, or was, and why he was carrying our name and address. The worst thing, the most suspicious thing, is this: whoever killed him, they stripped him of identification, everything, only they overlooked this one thing, this little piece of paper in the lining, so that makes it even more suspicious, you know, it's as if we were trying to hide the connection to him, and the only reason we didn't get away with it, was the fact that he had a secret hiding place, and we never caught on to it. That's what they think. I just know it."

I tried to show my sympathy. I made empathetic clucking noises. In fact, I *was* empathetic. It was a very strange story. "It's truly awful, Cynthia," I said. "And you're sure, you're absolutely sure, this was a total stranger. Could it be somebody you used to know, or Clyde used to know, or Daisy, and you all just forgot?"

"I swear it, Frank. None of us had a clue. I certainly didn't. But there has to be some explanation. Maybe he was some kind of crook, he was going to rob our house. Or maybe he was one of those people who steal identities, you know, they get your password or whatever. Really, I don't understand those things.

I keep reading in the paper about identity theft. They say it's an absolute nightmare. Once it happens, it's so hard to get things straightened out. Maybe that's the explanation, maybe it's identity theft."

I made some additional noises of sympathy. I had nothing to say. I didn't want to tell her, this seemed unlikely, this theory about identity theft. It didn't explain, for example, why anybody would want to kill this man, and try to steal *his* identity, or at any rate, hide it.

"Was he old, young, or what? What can you tell me about the dead guy?"

"Really nothing, Frank. He wasn't old. I told you, maybe in his 30's or 40's. I didn't really look very hard, it was such an awful experience. He looked ... ordinary. Well, as ordinary as a dead person can look. I didn't notice anything special."

I wanted to ask about marks or scars, or anything along those lines, or what kind of clothes he was wearing; but I guess they don't wear clothes in the morgue. I wanted to ask, but I didn't. I had to admit I was curious. In a detective story, there would surely be something distinctive about the man—a missing thumb, or some dramatic scar.

"Frank, I'm telling you all this," she said, "because I need your help."

"Me, Cynthia? Of course, I'd love to help you, but what kind of help?"

"Well, you're a lawyer, Frank."

"Yes I am. But I'm not a *criminal* lawyer; and, really, even if I was, I'm not sure what needs to be done."

"Frank, we need help. We need to find out who this man was. And why he was doing this awful thing. Maybe you have access to police files, really, I mean, you're a member of the Bar, or maybe you know people.... I just thought ... since you're our lawyer.... maybe you could think of something to do, anything at all."

I suggested meekly she might want to hire a private detective. I was walking a delicate line. I wanted to make it clear I had no wish to get involved—that's putting it mildly—but at the same time, I wanted to make this point gently enough so as not to offend a client, which she was. I thought I had succeeded, but as you will see, I was wrong.

I ended up giving her the name of a criminal lawyer—Nolan of course—just in case she might need one. I'm sure she found our whole conversation something less than satisfying. I did think, naively enough, that this was the last I would hear of this affair. Not that I wasn't curious—who *was* this corpse in Lytton Park? And why *did* he have Cynthia's address and phone number? But I imagined it would all come clear very soon. I expected to read in the paper how the police had identified this man, and what it was all about. But the affair turned out to be much more complex than I expected. And it got worse, much worse, as it went along.

2

It was Cynthia who had come to see me, but of course, the address and phone number didn't belong just to her, it belonged to the whole family. And it was the family that got me involved in their affairs—in fact, the very next day. This time it was Daisy, Cynthia's sister. She called me and said: "Frank, I have to talk to you."

I said: "oh," and it must have sounded funny, because she added: "It has nothing to do with what Cynthia told you yesterday. It's something my father-in-law asked me about; can I come see you?"

I had met Daisy a few times before. She was a few years younger than Cynthia; she had dark, somewhat frizzy hair, and she was, to my tastes, a little too thin. I suspected that Cynthia had at least a minor case of distorted body image, that she was borderline anorexic. It's something I'm sensitive about. Not about myself; if I have distorted body image, it's in thinking I'm thin, not fat. But I have teenage daughters, who gorge on junk food and then go on ridiculous diets.

Daisy probably never ate enough to put much meat on her bones. Maybe that's why she never had children. I read about that somewhere. The ones that starve themselves stop having periods.

I don't want to suggest that Daisy was really an anorexic. Just very thin. And she seemed upset—as upset as Cynthia, if not more so. Unlike Cynthia, though, Daisy always seemed upset. The few times I saw her, I can't remember her smiling. She seemed to be lost in a permanent world of darkness. How

Clyde dealt with that, I have no idea.

We exchanged a few words about the weather, and then I asked her how her father-in-law was doing. The minute I asked it, I was sorry. I had drafted his will, just some months before. He was after all a man in his 80's, and I didn't want her to think I was waiting for him to die so I could handle his estate. It was not that big an estate. His biggest asset had been the house he lived in, and years before, he had deeded it over to his children. He had some savings, to be sure, and some investments. But he was hardly rich.

"Oh, I think he's doing as well as you could expect," she said. "Of course, he's very old, and he has trouble walking, arthritis, it's painful, and it limits him; and he has high blood pressure, and other things, too: Parkinson's for one. Thank God it's an early stage. He's still very sharp. His mind is as clear as a bell. But really, it's not him I want to talk about; this is about his older brother, uncle Zack. Well, he's not really my uncle, he's Clyde's uncle, but we all call him uncle Zack. He's a widower, like my father-in-law, the men in that family live a long time, I think he's in his late 80's, he's got his own place, it's a small cottage really. He had a son and a daughter, but they live in Australia, they've been there for years and years, they have families, they don't have much money, and they almost never visit him. The point is, they're useless. And, Frank, to be honest, Zack—I think he's ... losing it, I think it's early Alzheimer's. Can't remember dates, and has trouble with names, he forgets things—you know how that is."

"Sad," I said. "Happens a lot...."

"He's always been very independent," she said. "But now.... I hate to think how he's managing. Well, we found out, he's not paying his electric bills, telephone bills, he doesn't go out of the house much, but the house is a mess, he never wanted to pay for a cleaning service.... and now he's lost his checkbook, he says. It's a real problem."

I nodded my head. I could see where this was going.

"My father-in-law needs ... well, maybe some kind of guardian, or some arrangement, something to help Zack out. But Zack is *so* stubborn; and he's so used to being on his own, he doesn't like to be dependent. But really, it's a crisis.... I don't want you to think it's about the money; he's got a little bit, nothing much, a work pension, and social security. This cottage, he owns it, the mortgage is paid off, but I don't know how valuable it is. Maybe he has some money in the bank. This guardian idea—how would we go about this?"

"Well, there are procedures," I said. "Power of attorney, for one thing.... And, if worst came to worst, you *could* have a kind of guardian. It's called a conservator, in California. But you know," I said, "a lot of old people, they really resent it, if you suggest they're losing it. Even when they *are* losing it. And from what you say, Zack could be just the type."

"Oh, that's so true! Zack would be furious, if we even suggested it.... But, I said, there's something of a crisis ... and in a way it's our fault.... We told him, why don't you have at least some kind of housekeeper, somebody to help you manage. Well, he didn't like the idea, and the house, it was turning into more and more of a pigpen; we said to him, look Uncle Zack, is it the money? If somebody comes in, keeps the place clean, helps you make dinner, what's wrong with that? Finally, he agreed, reluctantly, and we were taking steps, calling an agency. And then Zack said, never you mind, I did it myself."

"He hired somebody?"

"He did. *How* is another question; there was something really fishy about it, Frank. We just couldn't imagine Zack actually making these arrangements. But there she was. It's a Russian woman, her name is Anna, and he said, she's going to come in and clean and so on. And we were surprised, but we said, OK. But now—well, things are different....."

"Different? In what way?"

"Well, she's more than a cleaning-woman now. Suddenly, she's living there, in the spare room, and.... she's doing a lot more than cleaning, she's taken over, and, and he's.... totally dependent on her now, and we're scared. Oh, I'm not talking about sex, the man is as old as the hills, he can barely walk, but she's sort of a dominant personality, and I think she's starting to run things, and not in a healthy way. She manages his bank account, she pays the bills, and he seems, well, almost frightened of her.... It's getting to be pretty ugly, and we're worried, Clyde and I, we don't like this woman, we don't trust her."

"Well, why don't you fire her?"

"Fire her? How?"

"Well, where did she come from? Some agency? Call them, and say, she isn't working out, and that's the end of it."

"But ... it wasn't like that," she said. "She didn't come from an agency."

"Well, where did he get her?"

"That's even stranger. Actually, it was Edgar."

"Edgar?"

"Edgar Greenhouse. You know, Cynthia's ex-husband."

"How did *he* get involved?"

"I'm not really sure. When we asked Zack, he said, I got her from Edgar.... and we thought, what is this all about? And yet, somehow Edgar found out we needed somebody, and he arranged this whole business. So Clyde called him up, and said, what's going on, and he said, yes, he did this, because he had just the person for Zack, a Russian immigrant, she's strong and hard-working, he said, and she needs a job, and Zack liked her, and that was that. But now it's turned into a nightmare."

"Well, did you complain to Edgar?"

"I wanted to," she said, "but Clyde said it was impossible, and anyway, Edgar had no control over the situation, not anymore, he just found the woman, we'd have to get rid of her ourselves. And we'll do that, but we need your help."

"What sort of help?"

"Can you talk to him? To Zack? Like I said, he seems almost scared of her. And when we go there, she's always around, this Anna, she stands there in the room, and we have to ask her to leave if we want to talk to Zack in private. I'd like you to draw up papers, eventually, you know, papers about this guardian thing; but for now, if you could persuade Zack to get rid of this woman, and then, we could hire a housekeeper, and also get a real guardian appointed, somebody we can trust, Cynthia maybe. Or Clyde."

"I don't know. It's a tricky issue. Either Zack agrees or,

well, we have to go to court, and that can get pretty nasty."

"Please, Frank. Promise you'll try. Just a conversation. We'll pay you, of course, for your time. And, if he agrees, and we set the thing up, of course you'll take care of it, the legal arrangements, and all the details."

I was unhappy about the idea, but I don't normally turn down clients, and I did have experience with conservatorships, and durable powers of attorney, and so on, so I'm not a stranger to what's now called elderlaw. I agreed, then, to do what was necessary. And, like Daisy, I felt that something about the whole affair smelled bad. And I couldn't imagine why Edgar had gotten involved. In time, I would find out that things were even worse than we thought. But that came later.

Daisy said: "Frank, I'm so glad you're willing to do this. I'll talk to Zack, we'll set up an appointment."

* * *

Daisy was as good as her word, and I was scheduled to meet with old Zack on the weekend. It was not as if *he* had a busy schedule, but I did. Cynthia and Daisy suggested I come to their house, and talk to Mose before the visit. Mose knew more about his brother than anybody, and presumably knew how to handle him.

After work, that afternoon, I drove over to the house where Cynthia and the rest of the Winters family lived. It was a big, rambling affair, all dark wood, with a shingled roof. You entered a poorly lit living room, filled with old furniture, with a slightly musty air. It was a three story house, built about a hundred years ago. I had never been upstairs, but I imagine there were quite a number of bedrooms. In the back was a large, slightly overgrown garden. It looked like it needed more care than it got. In the back of the garden was a tool-shed, made out of what seemed to be old rotting planks.

It was the sort of house you considered either charming or gloomy, depending on your taste. I rather liked it.

Mose was an impressive old man, with snow white hair, a little cranky, but otherwise rather likeable. He was sitting bolt upright on a sofa when I arrived. Normally, he was in a wheelchair, but Daisy said he hated to be seen in it. He was as thin as a rail, with long bony fingers. He had a sharp nose, and very prominent eyebrows.

He had been some sort of engineer before he retired. He had a mild case of Parkinson's disease, as Daisy had said, and his hands trembled somewhat, even when they were folded in his lap. "I've got this damn Parkinson's," he said. "In the end, it'll kill me, but I'm putting up a fight. High blood pressure, too," he said, "I'll give you more details, if you want to hear what we old folks call the organ recital. But I'm not complaining. Well, I am; but I'm not as bad as a bunch of the others. I'm too old and feeble to do the dishes and mow the lawn, but otherwise I take care of myself, I can even put on my socks, that doesn't seem like a big deal to you, but believe me, half of the people I see at the senior center can't manage it. If they even know how. Half of them are completely demented."

"Mose," Daisy said, "you know you almost never go there. The senior center."

"Damn right. I tried it a few times. My sons talked me into it. I went there, and they treated me like an infant. Like I was demented like the rest of them. And what would I do there? Watch TV? Play bingo? No thank you. I'm not that bad off, right? I can still drive. The kids complain, they say I'm a menace, but what the hell, I don't do highways, and I don't drive at night. I've got a handicapped sticker. Comes in mighty handy."

Mose loved to talk. When he got a chance.

"I've got a good family here," he said. "I don't have any chores to do around the house, not that I'd be any good at it. I just read, and watch TV.... I get bored sometimes, but what can I do? I used to play chess, but my buddies all died on me, so here I am. My sons are good to me. Have you met Claude?"

"Oh, yes."

"He's my pride and joy. Daisy hates it when I say that. Clyde's a good boy. Too good. Anyway, I don't even need the boys. Daisy is like a daughter to me. She and her sister take very good care of me. I've got my own daughter, but she's far away, she's useless, and she's married to the most boring guy I ever met. The kind that wears starched shirts. Why she ever married him, I have no idea. To think of him actually screwing, like normal people, is worse than ridiculous, it's obscene. He's bald and ugly, too. Anyway, she knows what I think. She never visits me."

Daisy looked upset; it wasn't clear why. Because of what Mose said about his daughter? Or what he said about her husband? His obvious preference for the twin? I wondered. Cynthia, who was there, interrupted, "Mose," she said, "behave yourself. And don't talk so much, you'll bore Frank to death."

"I'm not worried about boring him," Mose said, "I'm worried about his fees. He charges by the hour, I suppose. I could tell him my life-story, but it would cost me a fortune."

"Come on," I said, "don't be ridiculous, Mose. I don't charge anything, unless we're actually talking business."

I'm not sure what Mose defined as business, but we did talk a little about Zack. "We're brothers," Mose said, "but he's a lot older. That's one thing. For another, we're as different as night and day. He's as stubborn as a mule; and besides, he's a goddamn fool, which I never was. And he talks too much. But never mind, we all do that."

Daisy brought in coffee, and some delicious pastries, which I found irresistible. You don't refuse pastries from clients. Meanwhile, Mose talked about ways to approach his brother, and then launched into a tirade about local politicians, the zoning laws, traffic in downtown Palo Alto, global warming, and the banking industry. This was pretty much a monologue. But after a while, somehow, the discussion turned to the dead man in Lytton Park, the man who, inexplicably, carried with him their address and phone number.

"Damnedest thing," Mose said. "A complete stranger. Never laid eyes on him. Nobody recognized him. They went to the morgue, you know."

"You didn't go, though," I said.

"No, thank God. Who needs that? I go to enough funerals, I don't need more dead bodies. They did show me a picture. Police made a photograph. They're going to advertise or something, try to find out who he is. They gave us some of these photographs, they said, maybe this'll refresh your memory. They thought we were lying. They don't trust anybody. Anyway, maybe you want to see what he looks like. We've got the picture right here somewhere. Cynthia, go get that photo."

I didn't particularly want to see it. I imagined some awful wound, plus bulging eyes, and that terrible stare dead people have. But they seemed eager to show me this prized possession, this object of mystery, and I didn't resist.

"Here it is."

I looked at the photograph. I stared at it, in fact. It was a man in his 30's or 40's, as they said. He could have been a bit younger. He was dark, maybe Italian looking, with a hooked nose and thick lips, but still vaguely handsome, though indisputably dead. My main reaction was one of shock and horror.

"Cynthia," I said, "this is really weird. I sort of know this man."

"*You* Frank. Oh God. Who is it?"

"I don't know his name. Or anything about him. I ... I saw him at a restaurant. He seemed to be drunk, or unruly, he made a scene, that's why I noticed him."

"A restaurant? What restaurant? Where, Frank, and when?"

"Don't crowd me, Cynthia, let me think. I can't remember the date. It wasn't that long ago. Maybe a month or so. I was with Celia, we were having dinner. The man was sitting at the bar. It's an Italian restaurant, it's called Zuppa Zuppa. It's in downtown Palo Alto, it's on University Avenue. Celia and I like the place, and it's owned by a client, Joe Zingarelli. We go there once in a while. Zingarelli gives us a free dessert. Mostly tiramasu. Celia can't stand it, but it's something I really like."

Cynthia seemed annoyed. "Frank, I don't care about your dessert. This is terribly important. You saw this man? What was he doing there?"

"Cynthia, how would I know? I didn't actually notice him at first. We had a table near the bar, it was really crowded that night, Joe usually gives us a better table, but this was all he had. He said, business is great tonight, Frank—usually he tells me it's lousy, he likes to complain, but that night even he had to admit the place was crowded. I think there was a big group, took up a lot of space, maybe some kind of celebration, noisy people. Anyway, Joe said, Frank, there's nothing much available, except here, near the bar. Well, we took it. It's really noisy there too, and the TV was on, some sports thing. We hadn't ordered yet, Celia asked for a glass of white wine, I had a beer. Then this guy, I hadn't noticed him before, but he got up, near the bar, or by the bar, and seemed to be staring at somebody, and started shouting, something about somebody stealing something, I really didn't hear it, you know, you get all embarrassed, and he was shouting and shouting, and then some waiters came, and he got quiet, and I think they persuaded him to leave; anyway, clearly he was drunk, completely drunk, and we all figured, that must be the problem, he's just stinking drunk. They hustled him out of there."

"And that's it?"

"Basically. It was all pretty upsetting. Celia said, let's go someplace else, but I thought that was cowardly; and besides, as I said, Joe was my client. So we stayed, and had dinner there. Funny thing, a short time later, I saw Claude, your brother-in-law."

"Claude?"

"Yeah. I remember, he seemed breathless, and he said hello, but didn't stop to talk. He sat down at a table not too far from us, there was a woman there, she was obviously waiting for him. He was late I guess, and he seemed a bit upset. I think he had just come in, or he had been in the men's room, I don't know. I asked him whether he saw this incident, I said, there was this drunk guy, and there was a rumpus, and the guy was yelling and screaming; but Claude said he didn't see it at all, he said to me, maybe it was before I came in. But this woman, the one he was with, she said she saw the whole thing, and she was extremely angry over something. She came over to us, we were having our free dessert, and she started in talking, and waving her hands, and seemed very excited; Claude said, leave them alone, but she said, shut up Claude. And she asked us, weren't we witnesses or something like that."

"Witnesses?"

"That was her word. Frankly, I didn't want to get involved, and I said, well, yes, we saw it, but what difference does it make? It's not important, just somebody who can't hold his liquor, it happens, and they had to throw him out. And she said, this is an outrage, I'm not going to let this go by, and I asked her, what exactly was the outrage, and it turned out, to her, the outrage, it was because they threw him out, and she got all agitated, and she said, this is becoming a police state, this is Californication—honest to God she said that—I'm going to complain, I'm going to find this poor man, he's a victim of brutality, people who own businesses, in this capitalist society, they think they can do anything they want to people, I'm going to get the ACLU involved, I'll put this place out of business."

"What did you do?"

"I didn't know what to do. I certainly didn't want her to make trouble, after all, Joe was my client, and I wondered, why is she so worked up? But maybe that's the way she is all the time. Anyway, Claude said, Sandra, cool it, why don't you, and she called him a coward, and a typical macho beast—I remember that phrase; she was really exercised about all this but she eventually seemed to calm down. Celia and I went back to our table, and that was that. Claude.... I don't remember what he did. This Sandra woman stalked out of the place, I think that's what happened. Anyway, that's the whole story; that's all I know."

Cynthia thought for a minute. Then she said: "Well, maybe this is something that might help us out. I mean, it doesn't connect this man with us, that's still a complete mystery, but maybe we can at least find out who he is. I assume you're going to go to the police, and share this with them."

I said: "Go to the police? I mean, Cynthia, why should I? What good would it do? I can't tell them anything useful, his name, or anything. All I know is that he got drunk and made a scene, and they threw him out of a restaurant. That's not much to go on, is it? And, to be honest, Cynthia, I just don't want to be involved. Now if I thought this would really help you...."

"But it *would*, Frank. We know where he was, on such and

such a day...."

"I don't remember the date, Cynthia."

"Well, but you know approximately. And maybe Celia remembers. Women are better at these things. And then, we know he was in Palo Alto, around that time anyway."

I squirmed. "Does that help us, Cynthia? Of course he was in Palo Alto. That's where they found his dead body. We don't suppose somebody shipped it in from Keokuk, now, do we?"

She said: "Don't be sarcastic, Frank. He could have come to Palo Alto the day before they killed him. Now we know that wasn't so. He was here for a month or more. He must have been staying somewhere. So this is important news."

I saw her point, but I resisted. "Cynthia, to be honest, I just don't want to do it. And there were lots of people there at the time, in the restaurant. If the police circulated his picture, somebody else will identify him. That's for sure."

She was obviously very unhappy, and it isn't good to make a client unhappy. So I backed down—a little bit. I said, if she made a copy of the picture, I would take it by the restaurant, and I would talk to Joe Zingarelli. He might remember the guy. Maybe the man was a regular customer, I said. That seemed to mollify her, at least somewhat. She promised to make a copy, and let me take it to good old Joe.

* * *

True to her word, Cynthia brought me a copy of the photo the very next day. Armed with this photo, I made my way to the restaurant. I found Joe standing near the entrance, with a sour look on his face. It was about 7 o'clock in the evening. Half the tables were empty.

"Hey Joe, how's business?" I said.

"You got eyes? Take a look. Business is lousy. Used to be, this time of day, you couldn't get in, they'd be standing at the door, the place would be jammed. Now, I don't know. I think, it's this damn economy. People don't eat out, they're scared. They think, they're gonna lose their jobs. Hey, maybe they will, you know? Some of the guys who work here for me, *they're* gonna lose their jobs. I give them until Christmas, then out they go. I'm not running a charity here. I got my own family to feed."

I mumbled something about how sorry I was. I didn't remind him he had been complaining about business for twenty years; he even complained in the so-called good old days, when (according to him) people were dying to get in and couldn't get a table. But maybe he was right this time, like the boy who cried wolf. He would, I hoped, somehow get through this bad patch and survive. I liked the free desserts. And I hate to lose a client to the bankruptcy lawyers.

In general, I love Italian food. It sticks to your ribs. I love olive oil, too. And tomato sauce. And pasta. Pasta is one of God's great gifts to the world. Maybe the Italians got it from the Chinese, I heard that somewhere. They say, Marco Polo found noodles in China, and brought them back with him. I don't really believe this story, and anyway, so what? To me, pasta is quintessentially Italian.

"You want a table, Frank? You hungry? I got a special today, swordfish," Joe said. "Really good, I wouldn't lie to you. I had some myself."

I told him this was a business call, and I was sorry, but I couldn't stay for dinner, Celia was expecting me. Anyway, swordfish is far too healthy. I go to his place for the pasta.

I read that swordfish is an endangered species. So we weren't supposed to eat it. Or was it something to do with mercury? I can't remember.

"What kind of business, Frank? Legal business?."

"Sort of, Joe. Can we talk somewhere, in private?"

He took me to a tiny office, in the back of the restaurant, near the restrooms. Inside were two chairs, and a small desk covered with bills and other papers. There were posters on the wall, mostly pictures of Tuscany; and on the desk, a large and old photograph of his wife and their four children, three boys and a girl, taken before Antonia dyed her hair and gained 50 pounds, and before the boys went away to college. I think one of them flunked out. Joe motioned me to a chair, and I sat down.

I asked him how things were going.

"Oh, so-so, Frank." He started complaining about taxes,

then launched into complaints about his children. "You got daughters, Frank? My daughter, Teresa, God help us; my wife, she raised that girl to be something, took her to church all the time. She went to the College of the Holy Cross, she got good grades—and look at her now. She's living in San Francisco, with this creep, he wears beads, she has the nerve to bring him around. I say to him, Are you a Catholic? He says, I'm a Buddhist. I said, come on, what are you really? He says to me, bold as brass, I really am a Buddhist. His name is O'Connell, and he says he's a Buddhist, can you beat that? And this guy is screwing my daughter. In the old days, a father like me, I would have yanked her away from him, put her in a convent or something, and beat the crap out of him. I thought Buddhists weren't supposed to fuck. What's gotten into kids nowadays? They've got no respect."

I made clucking noises. Actually, I was not unsympathetic. I have teenage daughters. The kids they hang around with, the boys with baggy pants—well, never mind. I'd settle for Buddhists any day.

Finally, we got around to my business. I took the photograph out of my brief-case, and slid it across the desk to him. I asked him if he recognized the man.

He stared at the picture. He turned it this way and that. He seemed to hesitate. He knit his brows and frowned. Then he said: "Naw, Frank. I don't recognize this guy. Am I supposed to know him?"

I didn't tell him the whole story, but I did tell him the man was dead, murdered, and that he hadn't been identified as yet; I said it was something connected to a client, and that this man had been seen at his restaurant. Joe was usually a voluble guy, very emotional, talkative, lots of grimaces and hand gestures, which wouldn't surprise you. But now he was strangely quiet. His face was like a mask, no emotion showing at all. I thought to myself: what's going on? Does he recognize the face, and doesn't want to admit it, but if so why? There had to be a reason.

I said, "I'm not saying you were a friend or anything like that. But, like I said, he was here in the restaurant, I don't remember the exact day." I went on to describe what happened, how the man was drunk and disorderly, and the waiters basically threw him out. "You don't remember that incident, Joe? It was pretty memorable."

"Maybe I do, I mean, Frank, I kind-of remember it, but look, it was a while ago. You been here Frank, you know what it's like when it gets busy, it's a frigging madhouse, and anyway, all kinds of people come here, you wouldn't believe what goes on sometimes. But usually ... I mean, this is a first-class restaurant, people don't act here like animals, I have good customers, executives come here, one of the Vice-Presidents of Google, he's here a lot, I got partners in law firms, they bring their clients, everybody loves the food, Frank. Some nights, there's lots of people at the bar, you know, waiting for a table, or just drinking, young people come here, like after work. Sometimes, some people, they have one too many, you know what I mean? They end up drunk. I don't like it, but I can't help it. So no, I don't really remember that guy."

He had to be lying. I mean, Joe runs a restaurant. Sure, there's a bar, and people do order drinks, but they come primarily to eat. Except for this dead guy, I never saw anybody drunk at Joe's. Not that I'm there that often. What I'm saying is, he simply *had* to remember this incident. I pressed him a little: "You do or you don't remember, Joe?"

"Hey, what is this, Frank, the third degree? I told you, no, I don't remember."

"And you're sure about this, Joe?"

"Hey, what do you think, Frank? Why would I lie? Anyway, even if I remembered, I wouldn't know his name, I don't know peoples' names, if they come in off the street, OK, the regular customers, I know some of them. My dentist, he comes every Thursday; and people who make reservations, they leave a name, they leave a phone number, but a guy like that, some-body who just comes in, sits at the bar, has some drinks; hey, I don't know his name, why should I?"

"OK Joe, I see that. But he paid his bill, didn't he? He was drunk, he must have had a whole bunch of drinks; did he use a credit card?"

"Frank, how would I know? Maybe he paid cash. Maybe he didn't pay at all, if we were so hot to get rid of him, get him out of the place, I mean, he was bad for the customers, you go to a restaurant, you don't want to see some drunken bum making noise.... And maybe he did pay, maybe he used a credit card, I mean, so what, a hundred people pay with credit cards, how could we tell which one he was?"

He was lying again. I can't tell you how I knew, but I was sure of it. Maybe it was the shifty look in his eyes. Who knows. Now, *why* he was lying? That was the question. I asked myself: should I report all this to Cynthia? Should I tell her there was something fishy going on, that Joe was lying in his teeth? But I decided not to. I had nothing real to go on. Nothing tangible.

Anyway, I got no useful information out of Joe. And that should have ended my involvement. This whole thing was totally mysterious, yes: a dead body, stripped of identification. And the mysterious connection to Cynthia or her family. But I'm not the police, I'm not a detective, I'm a lawyer in general practice. I told the whole story to Celia, and she agreed it was strange, it was puzzling; but it was none of my concern, really ... I had nothing to do with it. The best thing for me would be to stay out of it totally.

Celia has common sense. It's one of her best qualities.

Her advice was: keep your distance.

But I didn't.

3

A few days went by, ordinary days, filled with ordinary things, work, home, and leisure. I thought occasionally about Cynthia's problem, but for the most part I put it out of my mind. And some minor crises at home, and among my clients, occupied me the whole weekend. I had to put off the meeting with Uncle Zack. That was just as well.

A day or two later, Claude, Clyde's twin brother, came to see me. He had called first, and said he wanted to talk to me, about Zack, his uncle. I had hoped that this matter would die a natural death, but no such luck.

Claude, as I mentioned, was not the least bit like Clyde. I suppose, if you stretched a point, there was a certain family resemblance. But certainly not much. Claude was, to be frank about it, much better looking than his brother. He had dark blonde hair, blue-green eyes, and a dimpled chin. He was much taller than Clyde, and somewhat thinner. He had the look of somebody who exercised and took care of his body. But there was also a certain air of melancholy, a certain flavor of nervousness.... something hard to put your fingers on. Despite this, or maybe because of this, there was something appealing about him. My daughters would definitely classify Claude Winters as hot.

He and his brother were supposed to be quite close, although they seemed to me as different as day and night. Clyde was serious, hard-working, steady. Claude was none of these things. Clyde was, apparently, a one-woman man, happily married to Daisy. Claude had never married, but of course nowadays that has nothing to do with celibacy. In fact, Claude's history (I am told) was strewn with the wreckage of affairs; he had a string of women yards long. Apparently even Daisy, at one time. Cynthia told me it was Claude who introduced Daisy to Clyde. Maybe she was one of Claude's castoffs. Women obviously found him attractive. At first, anyway. Apparently, he had very little staying power.

Most of this was rumor, but not all of it. I got to know one of his ex-girlfriends, a woman named Marcia. She had inherited some real estate, and I handled her legal affairs. I won't bore you with details. Marcia had had no luck whatsoever with men, or maybe she had the habit some women have, of always picking losers. I couldn't stop her from talking about Claude; she knew I was involved, legally speaking, with his family. She and Claude had been a recent item. It ended badly.

"I broke it off," she said. "It was preventive, I could see it coming: he was getting bored and fidgety. He gets that way. My girlfriend Megan told me that, and she was right. He gets restless. Then he gets depressed. He gets these moods. Claude, OK, I have to admit, he's awfully good-looking, but that's about all.... I don't recommend him."

I wasn't about to recommend Claude for anything, women especially, but I nodded in agreement.

Claude was, I guess, still something of an open wound for Marcia. "He's supposed to be this macho man, and all that," she said. "But that's on the surface. Underneath, he's a bundle of complexes."

"Complexes? What kind?"

"Who knows? Or cares."

As I said, I did not know Claude well. I don't as a rule socialize with clients. It's a good rule to follow. Some of them, to be honest, I don't really like. I find them repellent. I don't mean physically repulsive. That's a problem for doctors, not for lawyers. I mean, most patients—my doctor's patients, for sure— are old people: women with sagging breasts, men who are fat and bald, with white hair on their chests; and even the young ones, the ones with nice bodies, they only go to the doctor when they're running a fever, or have sores dripping with pus, or a broken leg or boils on their bottom or god know what.

But I'm getting off the subject. I don't socialize with clients, as I said, but it's not an iron-clad rule. I also don't refuse an invitation, if I get one—that would be bad for business. Anyway, Cynthia was a fairly friendly client, and I actually liked her. She invited me for dinner, with Celia, of course. We went. It was hardly a highlight of my life, but we survived to tell the tale.

I don't remember what they served. The food was neither so bad nor so good that it stuck in one's mind. Cynthia tried very hard to be a good hostess. Daisy and Clyde were there; and Claude, and the old man, Mose. It was a pleasant enough evening, but somehow the conversation dragged. There were those terrible awkward silences. I find those so painful that I start babbling incoherently, anything that comes into my head. At other times, Mose went on and on about nothing in particular.

Claude hardly said a word.

Now he was sitting in front of me, in my office. He was one of these restless people, people who never really sit still. They move their knees, their fingers, their heads.

Claude got right to the point. He wanted to talk about Uncle Zack. He wanted to discuss appointing a conservator. Claude seemed serious, and troubled. Something, it was clear, was bothering him. Of course, the whole subject is unpleasant—old age, dementia, the decline and fall of the human brain and body. It's a nightmare for old people, and a nightmare for the young people stuck with them.

"You feel he can't manage on his own."

"We know he can't. He forgets things. He goes out for a walk, and then he can't remember where he is…. It's a real problem."

"And you feel this woman is … taking advantage?

He was quiet for a second; he looked down at the floor. I repeated my question, and he said: "Uh, yes, taking advantage. Yes, we do think so. We're sure of it."

It was striking to me that he always said "we," never "I." It was important to him, for some reason, to make this a collective thing. A family affair. I told him I had promised to talk to Zack, and he said, that was a good idea. Then I delivered a little lecture, on the subject of conservatorships, under California law, the rights and the duties, and so on. He listened attentively. I said, "Suppose that ... Zack agrees. And we go ahead. Now, we have to go through the steps I told you about, in court, getting somebody appointed to take over. Once that's done, well, the conservator will do the financial stuff, pay bills, make sure the bank accounts are in order, insurance is kept up, maybe even see to it that he goes to the doctor, takes his pills. It should be a family member, Claude, in this situation. There's not enough money to make it worthwhile, getting a bank in the picture, to take care of his finances; or hire a professional conservator. And I think he'd do better with family. Could I ask, would you be willing...."

"God no! Never! Not in a million years."

I was surprised at the vehemence.

"Then.... who?"

"I don't know. Maybe Daisy. Or Cynthia. Does it *have* to be one of us?"

"No," I said, "but it's better. Could be a friend, or a neighbor.... As I said, there are professionals, too. People who make a career of it, but I don't think, in this case, uh, it costs a lot; it's a difficult job, it's a lot of responsibility. So, family is better. If it's possible."

He lapsed into a kind of silence, and slumped in his chair. I couldn't figure out what the problem was. I could see why he had trouble maintaining relationships: he was a moody guy. We talked for a while longer, but the conversation was fairly unsatisfactory. We never resolved the issue, whether to appoint a conservator, and who it should be, but at least I felt the family was informed, that they knew the problems, they were aware of the alternatives; and the rest was up to them to decide.

Along the way, I couldn't resist bringing up what was on my mind: the corpse in the park.

He said: "Oh, that."

I told him about the strange coincidence, that I had seen the man, in Zuppa Zuppa. "You were there, too, Claude."

"Was I? I don't remember."

"The guy got drunk, and they had to throw him out. You were there with some woman. Or maybe you came in, right after this happened. Didn't you see the guy, the one they threw out—believe it or not, this was the guy who was killed in Lytton Park."

"Maybe I saw him. Maybe, uh, a glimpse. Why do you want to know?"

I said: "Just curiosity, I guess. You have to wonder, what's the connection with your family? Why did he have their address? It's got them pretty upset. You can't blame them."

He said nothing.

"It's a funny thing that I was there that night," I said. "And you were too. The woman you were with: what was her name?"

"The woman? Oh, her. That was Sandra Saunders. I was seeing her at that time.... well, she was a friend of mine. OK, more than a friend. But it wasn't going anywhere, and we stopped seeing each other. Maybe a week later, I'm not sure. I don't see her anymore."

"Where does she live? She could be an important witness," I said.

"Witness? To what?"

"Well, the incident."

He seemed uncomfortable with the whole idea. I tried to get more information from him, about Sandra Saunders, but it was like pulling teeth. I did learn that she worked at Stanford, that she was some sort of researcher, he thought she had something to do with the medical school, or public health, maybe gerontology; and he claimed he had no idea where she lived, which I didn't believe. I dropped the subject. He obviously found it distasteful. Do men in general hate to talk about ex-girlfriends? Claude apparently left behind a whole trail of women he had molted, or who had discarded him.

He said he would talk to the family about Zack's problem, and the conservatorship, and get back to me.

When he left, I decided to try to find, and talk to, the woman he had mentioned, Sandra Saunders. There was no problem locating her. Stanford University has a general directory, and I have a copy of it (a number of my clients work at Stanford). Sandra Saunders was listed, along with a telephone number.

In a way, of course, all this was none of my business. Still, she was some sort of witness, and she might have something valuable to say. I felt I owed it to Cynthia, to try to follow up any sort of lead. The police were surely investigating, trying to find out the man's identity. But maybe they hadn't heard about the incident in the restaurant, or about Sandra Saunders. And maybe these things would be helpful.

I called Sandra on the phone, the next morning, around ten, when I was reasonably sure she would be at work and answering her phone. She picked up immediately. Her voice sounded anything but friendly. She was one of these people who don't say hello, or identify themselves: they answer the phone with a rude sort of "yes?" as if to say, why are you bothering me.

I introduced myself. I told her I was a lawyer.

"So? And what do you want from me?"

"You ... you were in a restaurant, Zuppa Zuppa, about a month or so ago; and there was an incident, a man got drunk, anyway, they say he got drunk, and they threw him out of the restaurant...."

"Is he suing the restaurant? Is that it? He's suing, and you're his lawyer?"

"No...."

She said, "If he's suing, and you're a lawyer for the restaurant, I have nothing to say to you. I think what they did to this man, it was a total outrage."

"Oh, no, I'm not, really...."

"Don't people have rights anymore? What, is this a fascist country now?"

"Look, I'd just like to talk to you.... Ten minutes or so."

"What about? I'm really busy."

"It doesn't have to be right now.... I ... could come see you, maybe later today."

She agreed, a bit reluctantly. We arranged to meet on the

campus, at the coffee shop next to the main student cafeteria, at three that afternoon. I allowed myself plenty of time. Parking on the Stanford campus is an absolute nightmare.

It was a bright, sunny day, but in California that isn't news. I found a place to park a few blocks away, and I walked to the center of the campus, dodging bicycles. The heart of the campus is called White Plaza. There's a fountain in the center. The Plaza was crowded with students. Some of them were playing frisbee. Others were swarming around a make-shift booth, where they were collecting money or petitions for some cause; I think it had something to do with African refugee camps, but I was in a hurry, and I didn't stop to find out. Everybody seemed to be wearing shorts and flip-flops. I felt conspicuously overdressed.

The coffee shop was dark and musty. It was full of chairs and upholstered sofa-like objects. They were torn and ripped and shabby looking. Stanford University is as rich as Croesus; it has billions in its endowment, but students can make anything look shabby, even the Taj Mahal, when they put their mind to it. A number of students were sitting, drinking coffee, hunched over their laptop computers. Two bearded students were playing chess.

I recognized Sandra immediately. Her face was thin and pinched. She was drinking what looked like a cappuccino. She was, I would say, in her late 20's. She was wearing blue jeans and a faded peasant-blouse.

I sat down and said something pleasant about the weather. She was clearly not into pleasant. So I switched to the topic at hand.

"Getting back to that incident: did you actually know the man?"

"Listen," she said, "before we go any further. I don't know why I agreed to this, and I certainly don't have to answer your questions. And I still don't know what your angle is. You're a lawyer, you say. For who?"

"Well, actually," I said, "I represent Cynthia Greenhouse, and, uh, her family. I don't know if you know them...."

"I don't. Who are they?"

"Well, you know Cynthia's brother-in-law, Claude Winters. You were at the restaurant with him, that day, the day this incident occurred."

"Claude! Claude Winters? That asshole! What the hell does he want from me?"

"He doesn't want anything...."

"He won't get anything. I'm through with him. I don't owe him a thing. I don't care what he says. I want you to get that straight. Getting rid of him was the best thing I've done in years. All he ever wanted was sex. Some friend of mine introduced us. I thought, at first ... oh, never mind. He was a real asshole, let me tell you."

"Really...."

"Gave me a line.... Oh, he could talk all right. But it was all hot air. Oh, yes, he thought he was a real tiger in bed. He kept telling me, too, he was a big feminist, he believed in all the feminist goals, dismantling patriarchy, blah blah, but it was a lie, he was a big phony; if he was a feminist, I'm an Eskimo. And I got tired of his demands, and his moods. He was some kind of hypochondriac. Worried about this and that. Especially erectile dysfunction, as if I cared. What I ever saw in him, I have no idea. If this has anything to do with Mr. Claude, you can just forget it."

"No," I said meekly, "it hasn't anything to do with him, really. Miss Saunders...."

"Miss Saunders! Do you have to sound like a lawyer, too? My name is Sandra."

"Sandra.... The man, the one they threw out of the restaurant, well, did you know that he was dead?"

"Dead? What, did they actually kill him? I didn't think they'd go that far ... a bunch of thugs.... I should have followed up. I went outside to find him, I saw him in the alley, behind the restaurant. He was puking all over the place. I told him, he was the victim of brutality, the way they threw him out, and I told him he didn't have to put up with that. I said, I had my car nearby, I'd drive him wherever he wanted to go, but he refused. And that was that. I argued with him, but he insisted he was OK. So, look, I couldn't force him to let me help him. God! I didn't realize.... Dead! They must have beaten him. What did he die of, internal injuries?"

"No...."

"I knew this lady, worked in my office. She was in an accident, this other car backed into her car; she came to work, she said she was OK, just shaken up. And two hours later she was dead. It was internal injuries. She was bleeding to death, inside, and she never realized...."

"It wasn't like that," I said. "He died later on. In fact, he was murdered."

"Murdered! By the police?"

"Oh no—well, actually we don't know who killed him. They just found him dead, in Lytton Park, in Palo Alto."

"God, what a country this is!"

"But, can I ask, uh, Sandra, whether.... I mean, did you know anything about him? His name? Where he came from? Any details."

"No. Nothing. He didn't want to talk. I can tell you one thing: he wasn't born in this country. He had an accent."

"What kind?"

She said: "I don't know. European accent, I couldn't place it. His English wasn't perfect. Maybe he was undocumented. The way we treat these people, in this country, it's a scandal. No wonder he let them beat him up. I was thinking of suing that restaurant myself, I could get the owner in a lot of trouble. But, I couldn't do it by myself. I needed cooperation from this guy, this victim. And if he didn't want to, well, that was that. These people, immigrants, the ones without papers, they're afraid to complain. They know, there's no mercy, if the police get hold of them, or the immigration services. It's American fascism, I tell you."

"You never saw him again?"

"No.... Wait a minute. I did. Once. I was having coffee, on University Avenue, and I saw him in a coffee shop. I wanted to talk to him. I wanted to ask him, how was he doing, and so on. But he wasn't alone. He was with another guy. And I didn't feel like intruding. The guy he was with, funny thing, I knew him. He had been my lawyer."

This caught my attention. "Your lawyer?"

"I'm entitled to have a lawyer, why do you sound so surprised? You're a lawyer. I got a divorce a couple of years ago, and I hired this lawyer."

"What was his name?"

"Well, it's none of your business. But it's no secret. His name was Edgar Greenhouse."

Edgar Greenhouse! The name was like a bell ringing in my brain. Edgar Greenhouse was Cynthia's ex-husband. This was the first vague hint of some real connection between Cynthia and the dead man. The dead man had been somehow connected with Edgar. I felt a rising sense of excitement. If he had been a friend of Edgar, or Edgar's client, then Edgar must have known his name. This was something tangible, something I could follow up.

Cynthia swore to me she had never seen the man before in her life. Was she lying?

"And ... you saw them together? Did you talk to them at all?"

"I drank my coffee and got out of there. No. And I never saw him again."

I said: "This is quite a coincidence, Sandra. Edgar Greenhouse, well, he used to be married to Cynthia; she's Claude's sister-in-law?"

"So what? I never asked about Edgar's family. Why should I? I don't get chummy with lawyers. If you asked me about my dentist's family, I wouldn't know that either."

"But ... you said that Edgar was *your* lawyer, right?"

"I told you that already. Look: I had to have a lawyer. I was married to this worthless shit, God knows why women get married. I met him at a peace rally. His name was Borgo Fitzhugh, anyway that's what he called himself. His real name was Fritz, but he hated it. I don't know why I fell for his line. It was just plain stupid. Maybe I just wanted some company. We started going together, and he said, he wanted to get married, have kids, the whole thing. He was unemployed, said he was an artist, looking for work. He was looking for a free ride, that's what he was looking for. I had a job, he didn't."

"What's your job, Sandra?"

She gave me a piercing, and distinctly unfriendly look, as if to say, it's none of your damn business. But she did answer: "I'm a researcher. I work at Stanford, gerontology, you know, the study of elderly people. The way this society treats older people, it's a scandal. You wouldn't believe what goes on. People are always ripping them off. Their own flesh and blood sometimes. That's not what I work on, I'm doing work on memory, memory loss, and so on, but I'm not in the mood to talk about it."

"OK, OK."

"Anyway: I was saying, it didn't take me long to see, what a loser he was, what a lazy bum, my dear husband. That's what this society does to men. I won't say everybody. But most men. Borgo, he evidently thought life owed him something; for sure, he thought women owed him something. God put them on this earth to have sex with men and do the cooking. Me, cook? I said, do your own cooking. He was the kind of guy, if he lived in Arabia, he'd have me in one of those black things, with nothing showing but my eyes. He said, he couldn't find a job, and he was too busy with the peace movement. Bullshit. Anyway, I threw him out of the house, and I wanted to get a divorce. So I needed a lawyer. Frankly, I think lawyers are parasites, but the system has fixed it so you have to hire one, you have to waste your money, if you want a divorce. I know, somebody told me, you could do it yourself, you buy this stupid book, and it tells you all about how to do it. That's crap. It was like those manuals you get, when you buy a computer, some geek wrote them, they never help. Anyway, somebody at work suggested Edgar Greenhouse. I never liked him, he was an arrogant shit, and I was always smelling whiskey on his breath, but he got the job done. Not that it was hard to do."

"What happened to Borgo?"

"I don't know and I don't care. I'm sure he found some other woman to sponge off of. I don't even know if he's still around."

A small dose of Sandra Saunders, I could see, would go a long way. Did I have some lingering, male sympathy for Borgo

Fitzhugh? I'm ashamed to admit it. Of course I said nothing to Sandra. She rambled on for a while. But there was no more to be gotten from this source, and I left, with some feeling of relief.

4

After work, I had some spare time. Celia and I were invited out for dinner at eight, at a neighbor's; I took a detour on the way home and stopped in at Cynthia's. She had just gotten home herself. I wanted to tell her what I had found out. "There was this amazing coincidence, Cynthia. This woman, Sandra Saunders—she's quite something, let me tell me, a real piece of work, but that's beside the point. She saw the man, you know, the man who was killed in Lytton Park, she saw him at the restaurant, when he got drunk. I think I told you about this. Well, I went to see her, and she said, she had no idea what his name was, but she had seen him another time, and ... he was with Edgar."

"My God! Edgar! How come she knew it was Edgar?"

"He handled a divorce for her."

"But, Frank, what was this guy doing with Edgar? What's this all about?"

"Cynthia, believe me, I have no idea. But it's the first break we've had. I mean, Edgar must know who he is, what his name is, maybe he's a client. Why don't you get in touch with Edgar, ask him, tell him somebody saw him with this guy, and who was he?"

She was silent for a bit. "I can't do it, Frank."

"Can't do what?"

"I can't talk to Edgar. It's too painful. We ... well, I know, some divorced couples, they get along, they're friends and all that, but, to tell the truth, there's a lot of bitterness here. I don't want to go into it. I just can't talk to him."

"Maybe Clyde? Or Daisy?"

She said: "I want to keep the family out of this, Frank. I'll talk to them, of course; I'll tell them what you said. But could you—would you—do this for me? Would *you* go talk to Edgar? You're on good terms, aren't you?"

"Cynthia, I barely know the man."

"It doesn't matter, Frank. Please. Do this for me. Look: you're my lawyer. I'm hiring you to do this. Help me out here, Frank. I really need it."

Reluctantly, I agreed. I called Edgar's house. He wasn't in. I left a message.

The next day was a busy day for me—clients all day long. To be honest, I forgot to call Edgar again. When I got home, I remembered, and I called Edgar's number. Somebody answered, and I assumed it was Edgar, although it was an odd voice, somewhat childlike, somehow shy—I had a feeling, this wasn't Edgar. "He's not in," said the voice.

"Could you take a message? Please have him call me." And I left my number.

Then came dinner. It was a little tense. The girls were quarreling with each other, which was standard, and with their mother, which was also standard. I tried to stay out of it, but that was impossible. Celia hated it when I turned coward and refused to take sides. Of course, I had to take *her* side. She expected it. Anything else was condemned as "undermining her." In Celia's pantheon of sins, "undermining" was way up near the top.

I have to admit, she was right—her position was right—as it usually is. I should have taken a stand. I hate a fuss, but that's no excuse. I have obligations. Anyway, the meal was acrimonious, with a lot of uneaten food left on plates, some tears flowing down young cheeks, followed by ostentatious slamming of doors. To me, the slamming of doors was a welcome relief. The girls would stay in their rooms, listening to the awful music they seemed to like, and sending text-messages to their friends, explaining what beasts their parents were. I settled down with a book in the living room. Then the phone rang. It was Edgar.

"Hi, Edgar, long time no see. How are you?"

"I'm hanging in there, Frank. How about you?"

"Things are OK. Look Edgar, I need to talk to you about something."

"OK, what is it? A client?"

"Well, yes and no. Edgar, you must have read in the paper, about a dead body, how they found a dead body in Lytton Park, no identification—have you been following the story?"

"Not really. What's it got to do with you? Or me?"

"Well, you knew the man, Edgar."

"I did?"

"You were seen with him. Somebody saw the two of you, together."

"Saw me? Who with? I don't know what you're talking about. Who is this person? Does he have a name?"

"He doesn't have a name. I mean, of course he has a name, but we don't know what it is. He hasn't been identified."

"Yes, yes: but I mean, the man I was supposedly with."

"He was the guy who was killed, Edgar," I said. "So we don't know his name. We don't know anything about him. Only that he was in a restaurant, and made a disturbance, and they threw him out. Edgar, are you there?"

He was very quiet. I repeated my question. He said: "Frank: you say, somebody saw me with him?"

"I told you that. Somebody, I can't tell you who, it was in a café, on University Avenue in Palo Alto, and this person saw you there, Edgar, having coffee with this mysterious guy. So he's somebody you know. Knew, I mean. And that means you must know his name. It's no big deal, Edgar. Was he a client of yours? Somebody getting a divorce? We're just trying to get some information."

"What business is it of yours, Frank? How come you're involved in this?"

"I can't tell you, Edgar. Confidentiality—you know better than to ask. It's an issue with a client of mine."

"Well, maybe it's an issue with a client of *mine*, Frank. If it's confidential for you, then it's confidential for me."

I said: "Edgar, don't give me that crap. I'm not asking you for secrets. I just want the man's name. Besides, he's dead. Dead men aren't entitled to secrets."

Actually, sometimes they are. But this was no time to quibble about the ins and outs of legal doctrine.

"Edgar?" I said. "I asked you a question.

There was a silence at the other end. I thought I heard him sighing.

"Frank: I can't talk to you about this. Not over the phone. Please. I have to think. Don't ask me any more questions. There's.... there's a lot going on here. Murder is a serious business, I don't have to tell you that."

"I know that. All I want is the name, Edgar. It's not Rumpelstiltskin. Just give me his name."

"I ... can't, Frank."

"Can't? You mean, won't. Look: it's important, Edgar. You know it is. You said so yourself. This is about murder. Somebody killed your client. If he was your client. You've got to talk about this. If you don't, I'll have to take certain steps."

"What do you mean, certain steps?"

"Well, I'll have to go to the police," I said. "They're investigating a murder. They haven't gotten very far, I think. Anyway, as far as I know, they haven't come up with a name yet. I think you should go to them yourself, and give them the name and anything else you know. But if you don't want to go, well, then I'll have to do it myself."

He said: "Please, Frank." There was a kind of edge, a sort of desperation in his voice. "I need some time...."

"Time? For what?"

"I can't tell you. But if you're patient, uh, well, I'll you everything I know. But not on the phone. And not today."

"When then?"

"Next week. I need a few days. Can you come on, say, Monday night?"

I thought it over. Of course I could wait. I agreed. "What time Monday night?"

"Oh ... eight o'clock. Do you know where I live?"

I didn't. He gave me the address: 1257 Ruskin, in Palo Alto. I wrote it down in my little book; and I noted the time: eight o'clock Monday. I didn't know it at the time, but it would be an unforgettable evening. Not in a good sense, though.

* * *

The weekend was quiet and uneventful. I spent a little time at the office, on Saturday. Both girls had been invited by friends to sleep over. The house was blissfully quiet. Celia and I relaxed, read books, watched television.

I told Celia I was going to see someone Monday night, "client business," I said. It was not really a lie, but it was at best only half true. I felt vaguely guilty. Celia would never approve of this kind of adventure. As usual, her instincts turned out to be right. But I went ahead anyway. I drove to Palo Alto just before eight. It was a typical California evening, cool and slightly breezy. I was a bit chilly, so I put on a tan jacket, to keep me warm. Ruskin Avenue was near what passes for a downtown in Palo Alto. In Palo Alto, University Avenue is the nearest thing to a main street, lined with coffee shops, banks, and restaurants. Ruskin Avenue is located two blocks away, one of a series of tree-lined streets, with rambling older houses. Most of the people who lived in Edgar's neighborhood were rich, or else they were over 90 and bought their houses before the housing bubble bubbled up. Even after the bubble burst, these houses remained astronomically expensive.

It was already dark, and I had trouble finding the house. At night, it's always hard to tell one address from another, and I drove up and down Ruskin Avenue, which was very dimly lit, looking for 1257. At first, I couldn't find it at all; there didn't seem to *be* a 1257, and I wondered if I had written down the wrong number. I parked the car and started hunting, and I found my quarry. 1257 turned out to be a small cottage, behind a large, rambling house. Maybe 1257 had originally been a garage, or a garden shed, hastily converted into a place where students could live. In better days, Edgar would not have stooped to live in such a place, but according to rumor he had fallen on hard times. Liquor is expensive, in more ways than one. Most clients prefer lawyers who are sober.

I walked down a cobbled pathway, past the main house, and through a tiny garden. The main house was rather grand-looking. There were windows that looked out onto the pathway from the main house. The cottage stood at the end of the pathway. It needed a coat of paint.

I knocked on the front door; nobody answered. I rang the bell and waited. Nothing happened. All the lights seemed to be out. The lights were on, though, in the main house, which made it possible to see things better at Edgar's. There were no signs of life. Could he have forgotten I was coming? Then I noticed that the front door was actually ajar. Should I go in? Maybe Edgar had fallen asleep.

I had a creepy feeling. Definitely, the wise thing to do was to turn around, go home, and call Edgar some other time. Or go back to the car, and try his home number on my cell phone. But instead, I pushed open the door, which made an odd kind of creaking sound. It was pitch black inside. I have a tiny flash-light attached to my bunch of keys, and I turned it on. That way, I was able to find a light switch. When I turned on the switch, I saw I was in some kind of living-room. It was dingy, and filled with hideous furniture, cheap and gaudy: a few chairs, and two sofas that had seen better days. The walls were painted a sickly yellow, and the whole room had a pitiful look of neglect. Edgar had really come down in the world, but I knew that already.

"Edgar?" I called. No answer.

This was the second chance I had to turn around and go home. But something pushed me forward—curiosity, maybe. It was one of my bigger mistakes. Off to one side of the living room was a tiny kitchen, and to the other side, a bedroom. Still under the theory that Edgar was asleep, I tiptoed into the bedroom, switched on the light, and got the shock of my life.

Edgar was not asleep. Unless people fall asleep on the floor, with their arms and legs all twisted, lying on their backs, with staring eyes, and blood all over the place.

I was horrified. I stood there staring, paralyzed, transfixed.

Edgar was dead. I was sure of that. He looked absolutely dead. Dead as dead can be. Even so, in retrospect, I should have stopped, felt his pulse, tried to find out if there was any glimmer of life, and called an ambulance, called 911, called somebody—done all of those things, and, oh, yes, called the police and told them what I had found.

In a way, it didn't matter—the ambulance part, for sure. Edgar was irrevocably dead. That's what I thought, and as I found out later, that's the way it was.

And I didn't call the police. That was ... wrong, I know. But it was just plain impossible for me. Psychologically impossible. I wanted nothing to do with Edgar, with his body, with the police, or with *anybody*. I just wanted out.

For a short time, I stood there stock still, paralyzed in a way. Then I came back to life, as it were. I turned around, put out the light, and walked out of there, shaking and nauseated, as fast as I could, out the door, down the pathway past the main house, where the lights were very much still on, and where I imagined or thought I imagined somebody staring out the window, to my car, which I tried to start so clumsily that I flooded the motor, but fortunately, after about half a minute—it seemed like hours—it started up properly. I drove several blocks, weaving in and out as if I was dead drunk, then parked, got out, vomited on somebody's lawn, got back in the car, drove a few blocks, stopped and parked again. I waited until I got a grip on myself. More or less.

I must have looked like death warmed over when I got home, because Celia said, "Frank, what's wrong? Are you sick? You look awful."

"It's my stomach, honey ... something I ate...."

"Frank, I've told you a thousand times, if you eat fried food, and all those potato chips...."

I didn't have the heart to confess, no my dear, it wasn't potato chips, it was a corpse, a dead person, lying on the floor in his cottage, and staring at me with those ghastly eyes of his. But she accepted the story about my stomach, gave me something "to settle it down," and I escaped to our bedroom, where I stumbled over to the bed, threw my clothes off, turned out the light and lay shivering under two heavy blankets, trying to sleep and to forget this miserable night. With little success.

5

Leni Riefenstahl—if I have the name right—was this Nazi woman, Hitler's girlfriend or something like that, who made a movie and called it the triumph of the will. Something about Hitler's rally in Nuremberg, if I'm remembering correctly. They showed it in a film class I took years before, in college; but I had the flu and missed that session. So I never saw the movie. But the name stuck in my mind: triumph of the will. That's what I needed: a triumph of the will. After finding Edgar's body, I worked as hard as I possibly could, to forget it, to appear normal, to go on with my life. And I think I succeeded. Now there's a real triumph of the will.

I felt guilty about one thing: lying to Celia. She was so patient and loving and caring; she was very concerned, she said, about my stomach, and kept urging me to see a doctor.

"You really seem sick, Frank," she said. "You can't be too careful. It could be that awful thing that's going around. Half the teachers at school have had it. The other day, Gerald Gurvitch, the chemistry teacher, threw up all over his desk, right in the middle of his class. Then he passed out. They took him away in an ambulance."

"No, I'll be fine," I said. "It's getting better already."

"Whatever it is," she said, "you're asking for trouble, the way you eat." She brought up potato chips again. I swore I would never eat another potato chip, as long as I lived. That seemed to please her.

"Vegetable chips are just as bad," she said. "People are fooled, because they're vegetables, you know, carrots and things. But they're fried."

I had every intention of telling her the truth—but later on. When I felt up to it. I had had my spell of vomiting. My Gerald Gurvitch moment had been on somebody's lawn. Now, I was feeling much better; I was on the road to good health. Mental health that is.

It was two days afterwards that I saw in the local paper what I had been waiting for: a story about Edgar's death. "Area Lawyer Murdered," said the headline. The story described how he had not shown up at his office; the receptionist, Melissa Funk, was alarmed. This Melissa, it turned out, according to the article, was his "fiancé," whatever that means nowadays; and she had a key to his apartment, which is not surprising in the world of the modern fiancé. When he missed an appointment to see her for dinner, she went to the house, found the door open, and discovered the body. I wondered, when I read the story, whether she had vomited on the lawn. Probably not. I felt vaguely ashamed at the thought that I was so much less capable of handling this situation, than a receptionist who was also a fiancé. At any rate, *she* apparently didn't hesitate to act; she called the police immediately.

There was a follow-up story the next day. I gathered from it that the police had no clues whatsoever. Or if they did, they were not confiding it to the *South Bay Weekly*, the free throwaway paper I read. The cause of death was a bullet through the heart. The weapon was nowhere to be found. I also learned that Edgar Greenhouse was deeply in debt, had a drinking problem, had some ethical problems with the bar, and was, all in all, a total mess. Robbery had been ruled out as a motive; nothing seemed to be missing from the house. Having seen the house, I knew there was nothing to steal in the first place. The open door intrigued the reporter who wrote the story. "Did Greenhouse know his killer? Did he let him in?" The story also mentioned that Edgar rented a cottage behind the home of Sandra and Marcus Dillhoffer. Marcus Dillhoffer (described as a "junior executive in a software company") told the reporter that the couple had heard nothing. They had, however, looked out the window and seen a man emerging from the house, on the day Edgar died, and walking rather hastily—and suspiciously, they now said—toward the street. This had been about 8:30, they thought, in the evening.

Would they be able to identify this man? No, they doubted it: "it was dark outside, and we couldn't clearly see his face." All they could supply were a few rather general details. He was definitely male; seemed to have brown hair, was medium height, and was wearing a tan jacket.

The blood froze in my veins. The man they described was undoubtedly me, leaving the house in a total funk. And my fingerprints must have been all over the place. I had another panic attack. Should I burn the tan jacket? Or throw it in the garbage?

But then I calmed down. Millions of people had tan jackets. And my fingerprints meant nothing. I was not a convicted felon or anything of the sort, and I was reasonably sure my fingerprints were not on file with the FBI or wherever they file fingerprints. At least I hoped so. Did the bar association collect fingerprints? I had no recollection that they did. Probably not. I kept telling myself, I was safe, nothing to worry about. But I was still uneasy, as you can imagine. How could I not be?

6

I was not surprised when Cynthia called me the very next day, and asked me to come see her. I couldn't really say no.

I had no desire to talk to her. She was surely going to bring up the death of her ex-husband, a topic I wanted to avoid like the plague. Moreover, I was busy. I was working on a custody case, for a divorced woman client. The case was extremely complicated, legally speaking; and the personal aspects were equally tangled and intractable. I spent hours reading treatises and looking up cases on the California law of child custody. Later I was glad I had studied this issue so carefully.

It was getting dark when I arrived at Cynthia's home. Cynthia, looking frazzled and upset, was waiting for me at the door. We went into the living room; she offered me coffee, which I politely refused.

"I suppose you've heard the news," she said, "about Edgar."

"I saw it in the paper," I said.

"It makes me sick. Who could have done a thing like that? It's so crazy. It doesn't make any sense."

"The police...."

"Oh, I've spoken to them. You know, they wanted to talk to me, they asked me a million questions. I'm the ex-wife. Maybe they think I might have killed him, can you imagine? I suppose some ex-wives are bitter enough to kill.... I'm bitter, Frank, but the idea, it's so preposterous. Do you know, they asked me, where was I, that night, the night he was killed, or the day. I have no idea when he was killed, how could I? I suppose I don't have an alibi. I was at work part of the day, but at night, I was watching television. Frank, it's another nightmare. Why is all this happening to us?"

"Cynthia, I have no idea. And they, the police, they don't know who did this?"

"No. Nothing. Of course, there *is* one lead. The neighbors, they saw some man skulking about, but I guess that isn't much to go on."

Of course, I didn't dare tell her that *I* was the man "skulking about." And I wasn't "skulking," whatever that might mean. I was just walking fast. How that turned into "skulking," I don't know.

If only she had brought me good news—the police had arrested a burglar or a prowler or a disgruntled client, and the case was solved. But no such luck. I had a sinking feeling in the pit of my stomach that this was never going to happen. Never, because it was *not* a burglar or a prowler or a disgruntled client at all. Who then? I had no idea. Somehow, I was sure it had something to do with the man in Lytton Park. I don't really believe in coincidences. We knew there was some connection between these two men; and now both of them were dead.

I said: "Cynthia, I have to ask you a question, and don't get me wrong."

"That sounds ominous," she said. "What kind of a question?"

"You remember, we talked about Edgar and, uh, I told you what Sandra Saunders told me, you know, about seeing Edgar with the guy who was killed in the park, the one who had your address on him, when they found his body. You asked me to go see Edgar and ... I was planning to do that...."

"Naturally I remember. I wanted to ask you, did you do it? Did you get in touch with Edgar, and talk to him?"

Here I had to lie, or at least shade the truth a little bit. "No.... I didn't get a chance.... I spoke to him briefly on the phone, but ... well, we hadn't gotten together yet."

"Oh dear. That's too bad."

"Cynthia, I don't want to sound, well, suspicious. But it does seem odd, doesn't it? We find out Edgar knew this guy, the dead guy, and it's our first real lead. And now, before we can learn what, if anything, Edgar knew, about the man, whether he knew his name, and what sort of business they had together—before any of that, somebody kills him. That's pretty strange, don't you think?"

"Frank, you're scaring me."

"I don't mean to. But, really ... you see my point, Cynthia. So I have to ask you: after I talked to you about Sandra Saunders, and all this, who did *you* talk to?"

"Me?"

"Yes ... I mean, who knew about this business? That they were seen together, the two men?"

"Well," she said, "nobody really. I mean, nobody outside the family. I told Daisy, actually. And Mose. I remember telling him about it. But nobody else. Maybe this woman, Sandra Saunders, maybe *she* talked to people."

"I suppose that's possible."

"And Mose," she said. "He loves to talk. You know, he goes to the senior center, once in a while; he says he hates it, and claims he doesn't go, but in fact he does go on occasion. When he's in the mood. And, who knows what he tells people there."

I doubted any link to the senior center. I know the senior center; I had clients whose parents frequented the senior center. I couldn't picture one of the regulars pushing her walker over to Edgar's house and filling him full of lead. Or calling up the Mafia and ordering a hit on Edgar. Half of the people there have no short-term memory, and the other half have short-term memory but can barely walk.

Just then Mose appeared, in the living room, rolling in on his wheelchair. We exchanged a few words. I asked him, how his health was. "It stinks," he said. "You don't want to hear about it, it's too depressing."

"Sorry to hear that," I said.

"Never mind that. I understand Claude talked to you. About my brother Zack."

"He did."

"Have you done anything about it?"

I had to admit, I hadn't. "Not yet."

"It's a bad situation," he said. "There's this bitch, this Anna, big beefy broad; she's a Russian. She could be from the KGB, for all I know. She's got him scared and buffaloed, and she's just plain robbing him. Is there some legal way of getting rid of her, or do I have to hire a hit man?"

This didn't strike me as funny. "I think there's some steps we can take," I said.

"Well, take them then. Cynthia, did you offer this guy coffee?" She said she had.

I looked closely at Mose. He was a feisty old man, thin as a rail. He was ramrod straight. I noticed his sharp beak of a nose. He was bald except for a few wisps of white hair. His hands shook slightly; they were bony, and covered with age-spots. He was immaculately dressed.

"Pretty soon *I'll* be needing those steps. You'll have to get somebody to take care of me," he said, "I'm as old as the hills."

"Oh, you're not," Cynthia said. "You'll outlive us all."

"Don't bet on it," he said. "Anyway, I wanted to talk to you about something else, Frank. I might need to hire a lawyer myself fairly soon."

"Oh, really? Something about your will, Mose?" I said.

"No, the hell with my will. I'm writing a book, I might need you for a book contract. Do you handle that kind of thing?"

"Not usually," I said. "A book, Mose? Do you have an agent? A publisher?"

"You think I need an agent?"

"Publishers won't look at a manuscript," I said, "unless it comes from an agent. Otherwise, they'd be flooded with stuff. Every Tom, Dick, and Harry is writing a book."

"Well, I'm not Tom, Dick and Harry. Can you get me an agent?"

"I don't think so," I said. "I've never done this sort of thing. It's not really a legal job."

"It isn't? I thought it was. You always read in the papers, these movie stars, politicians, they get huge contracts; and there's always a lawyer, he writes up the contract."

I didn't want to point out the obvious: he was neither a movie star nor a politician. Instead I asked: "Anyway, Mose, tell me about your book. Is it a novel?"

Everybody writes novels. And nowadays, everybody, by spending a little money, can get their novels into print; the regular presses won't touch them, but they self-publish, or they go with a vanity press. They have dreams of making the *New York Times* best-seller list. Of course, they never get there, and in fact nobody ever buys these books, but the author puts copies on a shelf at home and then gives them out as Christmas presents.

"No, it's not a novel. Why the hell would I write a novel? Most novels are trash," he said. "There's enough trash in the world. My book is different. It's an advice book for people like me. Old guys. Really old guys. I call it, 'Life Begins at Eighty.'"

"That's, uh, a pretty good title."

"Damn right. I've got about half of it written. Cynthia and Daisy bought me a computer, laptop, they didn't think I could learn to do it, you know, you can't teach an old dog new tricks, but this old dog is different. I'm full of new tricks. Anyway, the book, it's got a lot of potential. There's books and books of advice and God-knows-what, for younger people; and all this stuff about how this one found God and the six people you're going to see in heaven, written by a bunch of phonies, if you ask me. But what about us? The people they call senior citizens? I hate that phrase, it's such bull, but never mind. You know how many old people there are in this country? Millions and millions. If they all bought my book, I'd be rich."

I had to agree.

"Look, if even half of them bought it, I'd still be rich."

Granted.

"Not that I'm in it for the money," he said. "I wouldn't throw the royalty check in the garbage, but no, it's not the money. I want the fame. You surprised? I'm a lonely guy. My wife is dead, God bless her. The kids are OK, but they have their own life. They tell me to get interested in stuff, go to the senior center, what am I supposed to do there, origami? Play Bingo? Half the people there are losing it, and the rest are boring, they talk about their gall bladders, pacemakers, prostate trouble. I haven't got long to live, I know that. Not that I'm sick or anything. But you don't live forever, that much I know. I'm 83. I've got enough money to live on, but I want to be somebody. It's my last chance. Look: an old geezer writes a best-seller, that's news. They'd write it up in the paper. Hey, I could be on Oprah. Something like that."

I had the feeling his chances were slim, but I kept my mouth shut.

"I'm an expert," he said. "How come? Because I'm old. I've got the experience. I'm *living* it, for God's sake. I can share things with people. I'm writing it for old creeps, men like me. I leave the ladies out. Let them write their own book. I'm no expert on women. I know, there's more of them than us. Most men don't make it to 80, they die off. The women all make it. Or most of them; there's enough widows around to reach from here to the moon. I know that. Still, some of us men are still alive, it's not like we're an endangered species."

I nodded. He went right on:

"I got a chapter, it's on sex and so on. I call it, 'How to Make Love when the Equipment Fails.' That'll get their attention. I'm trying to think up juicy titles for the chapters. Here's one: 'After the Funeral: How to Live as a Merry Widower.' And here's another one—I'm working on this one right now—I call it 'Deaf and Half-Blind: A Guide for the Elderly Driver.' I got one called 'Vulture on the Loose: How to Manage Your Heirs.' You could help me with that one, you know, the legal angle. Here's another chapter, 'Advice on Vice for Old Folks.' Hey, what do you think, Frank?"

"It's got potential," I said, weakly. He went on about the book for a while. Then, fortunately, we got back to the real business, which was Zack. I gave him a little lecture about California law, and the rules and practice of conservatorship. I pointed out, too, how difficult it would be to get the court to appoint a conservator, if Zack himself didn't approve.

"They've reformed the law," I said. "The guy—the one who, uh, needs help—he's got a lot more rights than he used to have."

"He doesn't need more rights. He's got too many as it is."

"That might be," I said, "but it's not easy. Do you talk to Zack? Do you see him?"

"It's an on and off thing," he said. "We're both old curmudgeons. Neither of us gets around that much. He's got me worried."

"Well, he's your brother," I said. I tried to persuade him to talk to Zack, at least on the phone, and he rather gruffly said he'd think about it. After this part of the conversation, I gave in to Cynthia, who was asking about coffee again; and while she was making the coffee, I mentioned Edgar's death, but Mose's only comment was that the world was "better off without that SOB." Then I asked, "Did Cynthia tell you about Edgar and the dead man?"

"Edgar and the dead man? What do you mean? Edgar's the dead man. I don't know what you're talking about."

"Sorry. I guess I wasn't clear. It was about Edgar and ... the man in Lytton Park. They still don't know who he is, as far as I know. But somebody saw him, talking to Edgar. Cynthia asked me to go see Edgar, find out what he knew. It seems he had some sort of connection with this man, maybe he could identify him, that would be a big help. But somebody got to him before I could talk to him. Somebody killed him. Now it could be a coincidence, Mose; it could be. Still, it's awfully suspicious. It's as if somebody killed him to keep him from talking to me. So I'm asking around, who knew I was going to talk to Edgar. And; well, you're one of the people."

His dim old eyes sparkled. "Yeah, I knew about it. Cynthia told me. She tells me lots of things. Are you saying maybe I killed him?"

"Don't be silly. I'm not saying that."

"You think I couldn't? Or wouldn't? The man didn't deserve to live, everybody knows that. Selfish, depressed, egocentric shit. That's what he was. Maybe I hobbled over there, or somebody pushed me in a wheelchair, and I went and put a bullet in his brain."

"He was shot in the heart."

"Whatever. I'm a prime suspect. When was it? Let me see:

was it two nights ago…. I was alone in the house. Everybody was out. No alibi. There you go."

I said: "Mose, be serious."

"Suppose it *was* me? I'd be hard to convict. Jury'd take one look at me, an old guy, I'd totter into the courtroom, or they'd wheel me in; they'd figure, what's the point? He's gonna die soon anywhere. Why send him to jail? He'll just cost the taxpayers money, doctor bills, and so on. Maybe I'll write a chapter in the book, something about senior citizens who kill people, or—wait a minute, it's coming to me, it's another chapter: 'How to Get Away with Stuff No Kid Could Get Away with.' I like it."

"Mose, please be serious. *Did* you talk to anybody?"

"Who remembers? I'm 83, maybe I have no short-term memory, like all the other people my age. The people in this house all knew about it: Clyde, Daisy. So did Edgar, don't forget that; he could have told everybody under the sun."

That was certainly true. Then Cynthia came in with the coffee, together with a very attractive coffee-cake, which I couldn't refuse, and didn't. At least it wasn't potato chips, though probably equally deadly. Mose took a piece too. Over coffee, there was some more small talk, but I left the house no wiser than when I came in.

7

I scoured the local papers every day, but there were no follow-up stories, at least nothing to indicate any progress, either with regard to the man in Lytton Park, or with regard to Edgar. I was dying to see a story telling me that somebody had been arrested. No such story appeared. Happily, though, there was also no progress in identifying the mysterious figure seen leaving Edgar's house, in a tan jacket, for which I was extremely grateful. The jacket in question, incidentally, was hanging in my closet, and nothing could ever induce me to put it on, for any purpose whatsoever.

I read Edgar's obituary eagerly. I learned that he was survived by two brothers, Roger and Martin, and that his parents were dead. No mention was made of his ex-wife Cynthia. There was information about the upcoming funeral, and I decided to go to the funeral parlor at least and pay my respects.

I put on my most mournful clothes. At the funeral parlor, there were a surprising number of people, grouped in little knots for the most part, talking earnestly to each other. I saw Clyde—but no Daisy or Cynthia. Clyde said that Daisy was home with little Clyde, and Cynthia "didn't want to come. She thought it would be hypocritical."

Clyde wandered off. Other than him, I knew almost nobody there. I was vaguely acquainted with a few fellow lawyers, who I saw, recognized, and nodded to. They were I suppose in attendance to pay their respects to a brother attorney. Probably they had some dealings with Edgar.

Then I noticed two people who I did recognize. I was surprised they were there. One of them was Sandra Saunders. Why was she there? The other was Joe Zingarelli. Joe gave me a somewhat embarrassed nod; I nodded back. I started to say something, but he clearly had no interest in conversation.

I circled around and came back to Clyde. He was standing by himself.

"I gather Edgar didn't have much of a family," I said.

"Well, he didn't remarry, if that's what you mean. And no kids. Must have had other relatives, cousins or aunts. I never knew much about him. Parents are dead. Two brothers."

"Are they here?"

"Oh yes," he said. "One of them is a lawyer, too; his name is Roger—that's him over there in the far corner, tall guy, sort of bald, in a dark suit.... Well, everybody here is in a dark suit. He practices in the Bay Area, maybe San Jose, I'm not sure. He lives somewhere south of here. I think he's married, and they say he has quite a good practice."

"Edgar was the black sheep of the family?"

"Well, that's a question. Martin is the other brother. He's over there, sitting down, sort of staring into space. He's kind of odd. The way I heard it, he was a brilliant kid, but a bit weird. He went to college someplace, then started law school, dropped out, and moved to Seattle. Never got married, lives by himself in a basement room, never spends a penny, works as a file clerk in some office; he's something of a recluse. Roger used to send him money, but he never needed it, he doesn't spend a dime. I can't imagine what his life is like. He used to visit Edgar. Instead of taking a vacation, he'd come and stay with Edgar. He did this even when Edgar and Cynthia were still together. He'd come and fix things that needed to be fixed, then sit and watch TV, never said much of anything. That's how I know him. He's really sort of pathetic. I have no idea what goes on in his head. Cynthia had a soft spot in her heart for him. It was like having a giant puppy dog around."

I wandered about a bit, wondering if I should introduce myself to the Greenhouse brothers ... or talk to Sandra Saunders, or to Joe Zingarelli. Clyde came up to me again, and grabbed my elbow. "Frank, see that woman over there? Don't stare, but get a look at her."

He was pointing at a large, somewhat heavy-set woman, in a dark print dress: a tall woman, perhaps in her early 40's; her darkish blond hair was gathered in a bun on top of her head. She looked somehow stereotypically Slavic, like a Russian peasant woman, or what I imagine a Russian peasant woman looks like. I have actually met zero Russian peasant women in my life. But I've seen them in photographs.

"Who is that?" I asked, in a low voice.

"That's Anna.... She's Uncle Zack's evil housekeeper. What on earth is she doing here?"

What indeed. Clyde seemed agitated. I remembered, though, that the woman had some kind of connection to Edgar. Clyde remembered that too: "Edgar got her the job. The job with Zack. But I always thought he had gone to some agency. Maybe she's divorced. Maybe he handled the case. Maybe she cleaned houses for him. I just don't know."

"She's not a cleaning lady, is she?"

"Well ... what's a housekeeper anyway? Just a glorified cleaning lady."

I wanted to tell Clyde that, on the evidence of my eyes, no cleaning lady, housekeeper, or anything even remotely similar had entered Edgar's house in the last few months; or if they did, they sat in front of the TV and accomplished nothing. Of course, I kept still. Nobody was supposed to know I had gone to see him.

I kept asking myself: why am *I* here? I wondered, too, when it would be alright to get up and go. But should I at least say something to the relatives?

In the front of the parlor, I could see the coffin, surrounded by a beautiful display of flowers, mostly white and red. The lawyer brother must have paid for them. The coffin was open, which I consider mildly barbaric. I dutifully joined the queue and filed past it. There he was, lying on puffy cushions. Lifeless, with that waxy look on his face. I really hate funerals, funeral parlors, and everything that goes with them. But because I do estates work, I have to go to a fair number of funerals. That doesn't mean I have to like them. I don't.

I found myself staring into the coffin, despite myself. I thought: just a while back, less than a week before, this had been a man, an actual person, a human being—OK, a depressed human being, a mess, drunk much of the time, unpleasant, living in a filthy, run-down cottage, but a person nonetheless. With everything functioning: heart, brain, eyes, ears, liver, kidneys, genito-urinary tract. A man who got up in the morning, went about his business, ate, took showers, made love maybe, drank a beer. Drank lots of beer, in fact. And whiskey. Now he's here, and he's a waxy corpse. How do they get that look? Do the funeral people put make up on these people? They embalm them, whatever that means. I decided on the spot to be cremated.

A middle-aged couple came up to the casket, and I heard her whisper, that sad old cliche, "He looks like he's asleep." Asleep? Not to me, he didn't. To me he looked dead. I've seen sleeping people, and (less often) dead people. This man was definitely dead.

An ancient woman tottered up to the coffin, looked in, and shed a tear. A younger woman held her arm. Somebody whispered in the background "That's Edgar's aunt." She looked 90, if she was a day. She also looked vaguely demented. The younger woman guided her away from the casket. Martin Greenhouse was sitting on a chair near the coffin. They went over to him, and he nodded his head.

What on earth was I doing here? I didn't even *like* the man. Was I supposed to say something to Martin, or to Roger? So sorry to hear about your loss, or something along those lines? And how was I supposed to identify myself?

The atmosphere was so solemn you could cut it with a knife. Employees of the funeral parlor, in somber black suits, stood around, looking as if they had lost their best friend, rather than having just gained a customer.

I sat down on a folding chair. A middle-aged woman sat next to me. She was overweight, with garish dyed hair, and she was quietly sobbing. "He was so fine," she said to me.

"Were you a relative?" I asked.

"Oh, no," she said. "I'm Dr. Planetree's assistant. The periodontist. He was our patient. Such a lovely man!"

I nodded my head.

"Dr. Planetree is out of town," she said. "I'm sure he would have come. Oh, we really liked Edgar. We did a lot of work on his mouth. He had awful teeth. But so pleasant. Always joking around. Of course, he had financial difficulties. That was so sad. I really felt for him."

I was amazed. People are unbelievably complex. This man had seemed a whole collection of faults; he was, by all accounts, seriously depressed, a man with a raft of problems, a drunkard, a man involved in God-knows-what, unpleasant, with a filthy household, a man who somebody *murdered*, a man without redeeming features—or so it seemed. Maybe his mother had loved him. Maybe the aunt, before her mind turned to mush. Maybe his brothers. And, for heaven's sake, his periodontist. His periodontist liked him. The dentist's assistant cared for him, too. He filled the dentist's office with a warm, rosy glow. He was able to vault past his liquor and his depression, and "joke around" in the periodontist's office, of all places. He was all sunshine while they were fixing his teeth. I couldn't believe it. Go figure. Life is truly strange.

Clyde was in the middle of a little knot of people. I decided that duty required me to introduce myself to Martin and Roger, express my regrets; and then go home. I started to cross the room, and I noticed that the two of them were leaving. Roger had taken Martin's arm, and was moving him swiftly toward the door. I don't know why, but something in their behavior seemed strange to me. For no good reason, I quietly followed them. They left the funeral parlor, and walked across the parking lot, toward a small park, which was just across the street. It was extremely dark—a cloudy night, with no moon or stars visible, and only a few pale lights in the parking lot. They walked briskly, and I followed them. If they saw me, I could always pretend I was heading toward my car.

They went down a path in the park, toward a bench, and they sat down. Roger looked around, but as he turned, I ducked behind a parked car; I don't think he saw me. I walked slowly and carefully across the street, just out of their line of vision;

and noticed a clump of bushes behind the park bench, where I thought—correctly—I could listen to their conversation, without any danger of being seen. I felt weird doing this, but at the same time, it excited me.

"Roger, I'm scared," I heard Martin say.

"There's nothing to be scared about. You just listen to me. Don't say anything to anybody. The police, nobody. You just keep your mouth tightly shut, OK? It's none of their business."

"I didn't kill him, Roger."

"Of course you didn't, Martin. Nobody thinks you did."

"Maybe she thinks I did. Melissa. She knows I was staying there with him. But I wasn't there when it happened, Roger. You believe me, don't you?"

"Of course I do."

"I swear it, Roger. Edgar, he said to me: Martin, I want you to get lost today. Go someplace. I don't want you around here. I said, where, Edgar, where can I go? He said, I don't care. Don't come back until midnight. I said why, he said, I've got people coming here, I don't want you to be around. I said, well what about Melissa. He said, she isn't coming today. He said, look, I have important business."

"He never told you what it was all about?"

"No, Roger, I swear. I'd tell you if he did. I'm so scared now.... What if they find out?"

"Find out what? Don't be stupid. You didn't do anything."

"They won't believe me. When I came back, Roger, he was dead, it was horrible, he was lying there, all blood and stuff, and I got so scared, I just ran away, I took his cell phone off his body, and I called you right away, you remember that, I was almost hysterical, I didn't know what to do."

"You did what I told you."

"I did, Roger, I did everything you said. I went back to the house, I put things in an overnight bag, and I checked into a motel. That's what you said I should do."

"And I want you to stay there. Don't go near his house. Do you have clothes and stuff there? In the house?"

"Oh God, I do."

"Doesn't matter. You used to visit him, and why shouldn't you have some clothes there? Anyway, we'll cross that bridge when we come to it. I'm trying to keep you out of this mess. After the funeral, I want you to go back home. I'll keep in touch with you."

"But she knows.... Melissa knows ... she'll tell them...."

"Leave her to me, Martin. I'll take care of her. Don't you worry. Hell, maybe she killed him herself. Maybe they had an argument. I never liked her."

"Oh, no, not Melissa; she wouldn't do that...."

"Well, Martin, *somebody* did it, right? *Somebody* killed him. Do you have any idea who?"

"Oh God, Roger, no. But somebody was coming to see him, that's why he wanted me out of the way. And the neighbors, they saw this man, they saw him coming out of the house; he must have been the guy who did it, maybe they'll find him, catch him, maybe they've got a description, I think they do. He was wearing a tan jacket, or something."

"Let's hope they find the guy. I wish I knew more about what Edgar was up to. He never confided in me, well, you know that. We didn't always get along. I have the feeling, he was involved in some pretty funny stuff. You were camping out there, did you get any idea, what kind of monkey business he was in?"

"I dunno, Roger. I never wanted to know. That woman, she was involved: Melissa. But I never asked him anything. Oh God, this is so awful. What's going to happen now?"

"Nothing, you dork. Just calm down and leave everything to me. OK? Meanwhile, I gotta go.... Remember: don't talk to anybody, and stay where you are. You got that? I'll drive you to your motel. Just keep quiet, watch TV, get a good night's sleep. And call me in the morning."

"I haven't got any money, Bro."

"What do you do with your money? You never spend it. OK, I'll give you some cash; the main thing is, don't worry."

That was the end of the conversation. They got up and left, heading no doubt toward Roger's car. I waited a few minutes, until I was sure they were gone, then I walked back to the funeral parlor. At the door, I met Joe Zingarelli, who was on his way out. He looked embarrassed.

"Hey, Frank, what's new?" he said, apparently trying to sound good-humored.

"Not much, Joe: say, can I have a word with you?"

"Does it have to be now, Frank? Remember, I run a business. I got to go back to the restaurant. When the boss doesn't show up, God knows what goes on."

"It'll just be a minute," I said. "Where are you parked?"

He pointed in the direction of the parking lot. I walked next to him. "Can I ask you, Joe, what you were doing here?"

"Same as you," he said, "hey, the guy was a customer, wasn't he? I got a right to go to his funeral. Why're you questioning me?"

"I'm not questioning you, Joe. Just curious. Do you go to all the funerals, I mean, funerals of customers?"

"Hey, Frank, not all of them. You worried whether I'll come to yours?"

I said: "Come on, Joe. I'm your lawyer. You can talk to me. Tell me what's up. This guy was murdered, you realize that, don't you?"

"Yeah, so what? I didn't do it. They saw some guy coming out of the place, I can't remember what time it was, but he's the one. Me, I got an alibi, if that's what you're asking. I was in my restaurant, taking care of customers. I got dozens of witnesses."

I found that curious. Why was he being so defensive? As if somebody might imagine he had a motive, a reason to kill Edgar Greenhouse.

"OK, Joe, I believe you," I said. "You're not the one."

"Damn right, Frank. Hey, maybe it was you. Maybe you killed him, Frank."

"Now why would I do that?" I said, trying to sound nonchalant. This whole business would be funny, if it wasn't so scary. Everybody thinks I *did* kill him—that is, they think the man who was leaving the house had just finished off Edgar Greenhouse. What they didn't know was that I was the mysterious "skulking" figure. What they also didn't know was that I was totally innocent. Whenever I thought about this constant harping on the dim figure leaving the house, chills ran up and down my spine. But in my rational moments, I realized I was perfectly safe. Nobody knew I had an appointment with Edgar. And nobody got a good enough look at me. At least I thought so. It turns out, I was wrong, but we'll come to that later.

"Hey, how should I know?" Joe said. "Maybe he owed you money. He owed lots of people money."

"Including you, Joe?"

He gave a hoarse, meaningful laugh. Meaningful, but only if you knew the meaning, which I did not. "No, not me," he said. "The opposite."

"What does that mean, Joe?"

"Oh, nothing. Listen, Frank, I really got to go. Honest to God."

I was getting nowhere with Joe, so I said goodbye, and walked over to my own car. As I was getting in, somebody tapped me on the shoulder. It startled me; I turned and looked to see who it was. It was, surprisingly, Joe.

"Frank," he said, "listen ... can we talk a little more?"

"Sure, Joe. You don't need a lift, do you?"

"Naw, my car's here, in the lot, remember? Look: I didn't want to say anything in there, or when I was by my car; somebody might hear, you know? And ... OK, that's not really the case.... I just didn't ... uh...."

"You didn't what, Joe?

He walked around the car, and slid into the passenger seat. Then he said: "Frank, I didn't want to talk. I just didn't. But I thought it over and—look: I told you a lie. I didn't want to get involved, you don't blame me, do you?"

"No, I don't blame you, Joe. But involved in what?"

"You know. Edgar. Anyway, you're my lawyer, Frank. This is all confidential, right? I'm not supposed to keep things from you. My wife, she says, you got a lawyer, you gotta talk to the lawyer. They take a vow of silence, lawyers. It's like priests, you know what I mean?"

"Sure, Joe."

"This guy Edgar, he handled my divorce, my first wife, she was a real bitch—it was trouble trouble all the way. Anyway, when we split, Brenda moved out, and she said she wanted a divorce, I think she had somebody on the side, but I couldn't prove it; anyway, I needed a lawyer, and this other customer, he recommended Edgar, and, well, it was before I got to know you, Frank, that's why I went to this Edgar."

"It's OK, Joe, I understand."

"Anyway: me and Edgar, we got to be friendly; we used to talk a lot, he had his problems. Drank too much, owed a lot of money; I don't know why exactly. After the divorce, he seemed to get worse, you know? I wanted to help him. He used to come into the restaurant a lot, cry on my shoulder. He'd come in, he'd drink, and tell me his troubles. Well, some of them anyway. I'm sure there was other stuff, stuff he didn't want to talk about.

"One day, I came into the restaurant, about 7 o'clock, usually I'm there earlier, but this time I wasn't, I don't remember why. I saw this guy in the restaurant, he was sitting in a booth with Edgar, they were talking, arguing, I don't know what about. Then, the next day, he came to the restaurant again, same man, sat at the bar, and I was there, you know, like usual. He said, hey Joe, where's Edgar? I didn't like his tone. I said, how would I know? He said, well, I was supposed to meet him here; I said, well, he's not here, so what? I didn't like the guy's looks, and I didn't like him calling me Joe, who gave him that right? Well, he started drinking and drinking, and that's the time he got so drunk, and we had to throw him out. I never saw him again. Now he's dead, and this woman, Sandra Saunders, she's a colossal pain in the ass, she's pestering me, she says she's going to sue me, make all sorts of trouble, because I threw him out, as if he was some kind of frigging victim, and I was a fascist, she used that word, I said to her, listen lady, I'm Italian, don't talk to me about fascists, I know all about fascists, Mussolini, he was a fascist, he was like one of those Nazis, I'm an American, I was born here, so don't you go calling me names."

Despite this river of words, I still didn't know why he came to the funeral.

"Well, she did go to the police, can you believe what that bitch did to me? Like I killed the guy, you know? She said I was a frigging suspect. That I had already had a history, you know, history of violence toward the guy, can you believe it? And they came and asked me a whole bunch of questions, and I told them, I don't talk without my lawyer, so I called up Edgar, and I said, you're my lawyer, these guys are trying to pin some kind of murder thing on me, and I don't even know the guy's name, he's your buddy, you've got to help me."

"And then what happened?"

"He freaked out, he said, don't ever call me again, not about this thing, he started yelling, and I thought, what's with this guy, he's lost it, maybe he's drunk, or nuts, or whatever; and I said, alright, alright, I just needed some help, and he said, don't mention my name, don't you dare ever connect me with that guy. I said, why should I? I don't know his name or anything, and he said, let's keep it that way. And he hung up on me. And now somebody killed *him* too. I mean, Edgar, they killed Edgar, too. And I ask you, Frank, what's this all about?"

"I honestly don't know. It's a real mystery. This other man, the first guy, the one in Lytton Park, you're sure you don't know his name, or his address, or anything about him? The guy you threw out, the guy who was killed later on?"

"Why would I lie? Tell you one thing: he had an accent, he wasn't an American, that's for sure. Some kind of foreigner."

"What kind of foreigner?"

"How should I know? Well, he wasn't Italian, I know that much. Maybe a Polish guy, something like that. My new wife's half-Polish, some of her relatives sound like that. Or he could be some kind of Arab. Who knows. He must have had something going with Edgar, but damned if I know what it is. If only that bitch Sandra would leave me alone.... Hey, maybe Edgar killed him, who knows? The guy in Lytton Park. Some kind of gang thing. And then they got back at Edgar, you know, revenge."

This came out in a rapid rush of words. Somehow I felt I wasn't getting the whole story, but I had to be satisfied with what I got. I reminded myself that Joe was a client. A valuable client at that. His restaurant, despite his bouts of gloom, made quite a bit of money, and he was thinking of opening a branch in San Jose. Opening a branch is usually a recipe for disaster, but until it failed, there would be a nice chunk of legal work for me. Not to mention even more free desserts.

Joe left the car, and I drove home, thinking about what I knew and didn't know about the late Edgar Greenhouse. And, from time to time, my mind turned to thoughts about Italian pasta and desserts.

8

We lawyers never get what's called walk-in trade. I have a stable of clients—none of them are Fortune 500 companies, but I couldn't handle a big company anyway. My clients see me by appointment. So it's unusual for me to come to the office, and find somebody waiting in the outer office, without an appointment. It happens from time to time, but not very often.

I was, to say the least, surprised, when I came to the office—a little late, to be sure—and found a woman sitting in the outer office. And when I went into my own room, she got up and followed me.

She was a woman of a certain age, as the saying goes. I would guess 45. She had on too much makeup, weighed about ten pounds too much, had dyed blonde hair with tiny streaks of brown in it and wore a lot of eye makeup. There was a toughness to her, a look about her face that said: I've been around. She had rings on every single finger, big fat gaudy rings, and several strands of beads around her neck. She was wearing slacks that were at least two sizes too tight; this emphasized parts of her body I would have thought she would be better off hiding than showing. There were definite signs of visible panty line. To me, it all looked unnecessarily garish and unattractive. But what do I know about such things.

"I'm Melissa Funk," she said, "I worked for Edgar Greenhouse. I need to talk to you."

I nodded solemnly. I remembered the rumor, that she and Edgar had been romantically involved, if that's the phrase to use, so I said: "So sorry to hear about your loss."

She laughed hoarsely. "Spare me the crap. I'm almost glad he's dead, believe it or not."

This startled me: "I'm sorry…. Somebody told me you two were, uh, well…."

"Were what?"

"Were engaged," I said. Of course, "engaged" is old-fashioned. I think nobody gets engaged anymore. They just move in with each other. Then they either marry or they don't. Most of the people I know don't have a formal engagement, there's no diamond engagement ring. Nonetheless, sometimes they do get married, eventually. Sometimes even a huge extravaganza, complete with bridesmaids and monogrammed napkins.

She laughed again. "Let's say it was mostly a business relationship."

"Business?"

"Edgar was involved in a lot of things. None of them were panning out, but he kept trying. I knew mostly what he was up to. Mostly. But not everything. For instance, I don't know what he had going with you."

"With me? Are you kidding?"

"I am not kidding. Why else would you kill him?"

I was thunderstruck: "What did you say?"

"You heard me. Don't play stupid with me. I don't have time for that. Look: I know you killed him, let's not play games."

"You can't be serious," I said. "That's totally ridiculous. Where would you get such a crazy idea?"

She leaned forward, and her tough face looked even tougher, a combination of her somewhat puffy cheeks, the makeup, the eye-shadow, and a certain glint in her eyes. She reminded me of old legends about dragons or basilisks or whatever, with tongues of flame coming out of their mouths. "Edgar told me about you. He told me you were coming to see him. You thought it was a secret? Well, you're wrong. I knew all about that. I didn't know *why* you were coming over; he said he'd tell me later. You went, and you killed him. You better tell me why. I need to know."

"I ... I didn't go," I said. A trapped beast will do anything to save itself from the jaws of a predator. A trapped guy like me will simply blurt out a lie.

"Listen, Mr. Lawyer," she said, "The two creeps who own the house in front of Edgar's cottage, they saw you leaving the place. You fit the description. They didn't know it was you. But I knew it was, because of what Edgar told me. You were seen, about eight o'clock or whenever. That's about when somebody killed him. So that means: you were the somebody. Don't give me a line of bull. I'm not buying your story, whatever it is."

I sat there frozen in terror. This couldn't be happening, I said to myself. Raw, naked fear must have been written all over my face, because she started to laugh. "You're scared," she said. "I can see it. But look, you don't need to get all in an uproar. I'm not going to tell, OK? I'm here to make a deal. Frankly, I don't give a damn why you killed him. I'm not going to the police, understand?"

"I didn't kill him," I said, weakly.

"Look, I need honest answers. Did you or did you not go to Edgar's house."

"OK, I did."

"And was it or wasn't it you, the guy those creeps saw leaving the house?"

I said: "Maybe it was. I saw a light in their window. But I did not do anything to Edgar Greenhouse. I never touched him. He was dead when I got there. He was lying in the bedroom, and he was dead. And I got out of there as fast as I could. Wouldn't you?"

She said: "No I wouldn't. And I didn't. When I came by, and found him, I called the police. You didn't."

"I was in a panic," I said.

She made a gesture with her hand, more or less indicating, that she didn't believe a word I was saying. "OK, that's your story, I suppose."

"It's not a story. It's the truth."

"Have it your way. Look: I don't really care. I'm here to offer you a deal."

"What … uh, what kind of a deal?"

She said: "You're supposed to arrange something for Zack Winters, am I right? A conservatorship?"

I was genuinely surprised. What on earth could Zack's mental state, and the arrangements for his care—what on earth could that have to do with Edgar Greenhouse? Or with this woman? "Well, yes," I said. "There's been discussions. With the family. But we haven't done anything about it, yet."

"OK: then don't," she said.

"Pardon?"

"You heard me. No conservatorship. Let things go on the way they are now, understand? I don't want you doing anything to upset the arrangement."

I was puzzled. I said: "What arrangement? There isn't any arrangement."

"I mean, just let it go. Let things go on the way they're going. No changes."

"But why?"

She said: "It's none of your business. Just do it. And then I'll forget about telling the cops what I know."

My mind was working rapidly. Old Zack and his affairs—somehow they were connected to Edgar; and to Melissa. And then, in some weird way, they must be connected to the man in Lytton Park. This had to be the case. But why?

Myself, I'm basically a coward, I have to admit it. I desperately wanted Melissa to keep her mouth shut. I didn't want anybody to know I had been at Edgar's house. I could just see myself behind bars, wearing an orange jump-suit, accused of murder. What a disaster that would be, for everybody. What would Celia think? The kids would be objects of gossip, and nothing is worse for a teenager than people snickering behind their back. And where would the money come from? Celia doesn't make that much, and my practice—it would kill my practice. And oh God, the things I read about prisons. They rape people there, there's gangs, and cockroaches, and people stick knives in your back; the food is inedible, and they don't let you go to the doctor. And all those thugs. I wouldn't last a day.

Poor me! Once the police think you're guilty of something,

you're in deep, deep trouble. Or had I been watching too much TV? I don't know much about real-life police. But I prefer not to know. I'll gladly forego any first-hand knowledge.

But if I did what Melissa wanted, would that make a difference? If I bowed out, if I made up some excuse and said, I'm sorry, I can't handle this, couldn't the family just hire another lawyer? Lawyers are a dime a dozen.

It was as if she was reading my mind. "I want you to do whatever it takes to stop the whole proceeding. Just quitting isn't enough—do you hear me? I want the issue to go away. The minute it doesn't, that's when I go blabbing to the cops."

"Make it go away: how can I do that?"

"That's your problem. You figure it out."

"Look, Melissa, be reasonable. If the family wants to go ahead with this, they will; they don't need me."

"I told you, you figure it out. Tell them why it shouldn't be done. Tell them it's illegal or something. They'll listen to you. And if they don't.... I know what you lawyers are like; I worked for a lawyer, don't forget that. You've got all kinds of tricks up your sleeves. Just do it."

It was no use arguing with Melissa Funk. I nodded, and said, I'd see what I can do. She said: "I don't want excuses, I want results." I could only repeat my promise, in a helpless tone of voice. She had made her point, and she left.

* * *

Just do it, she said. But how? It was easy for her to mouth these words. But not easy for me to accomplish. You can imagine how this conversation upset me. I had a desperate feeling inside. Not even junk food improved my state of mind.

Somehow I got through the day, talking to clients, working on documents—the usual. I unburdened myself to Celia that evening. The girls were off at friends' houses, doing whatever kids do at their age. I hoped that whatever it was, it didn't include sex; but I was too obsessed with my own problems to spend this particular evening worrying about adolescent girls and their adolescent boys. Celia and I went out to dinner, at a fish restaurant. Actually, I don't like fish; and I bitterly resent the fact that they are full of Omega oil, whatever that is, which is enormously good for you. Why can't they discover some marvelous properties in beef? Or chocolate for that matter?

I have a horror, too, of fish bones. Little bones that lurk inside fish, waiting to surprise you. I hate fish bones.

That night was mercifully free of fish bones. The night's fish was halibut. I told the whole story to Celia, and begged her for advice.

"Why didn't you tell me this before, Frank? Honestly, I just don't seem able to trust you anymore. It's shocking, Frank. That you would lie to me. I have to be able to trust you; that's what marriage is all about."

Of course, she *can* trust me, but only on very big things, like adultery (I never commit it), or finances (I value her advice). It's only on little things that I tell lies. I think it's an important distinction. But I kept quiet about this marital insight. Instead, I humbled myself and told her I was sorry.

I wish I could say that she gave me good advice. Often she does. But in this case, she could only confirm what I knew already, and what I was afraid of: I was in a spot. I explained that it would be unprofessional, and unethical, to try to talk my clients out of appointing a conservator for Zack, if I acted for purely personal reasons, and rather fishy reasons at that. Celia suggested that I might go to the police, tell them that I was the skulking figure, but that I had nothing to do with the murder. "That's the truth, dear," she said. "How can the truth hurt you?"

I wish that were true. Sometimes the truth hurts a great deal. I found the idea of going to the police simply impossible. Anyway, they'd want to know, why didn't I call them? I found a dead body, and just left it there? Maybe that was some sort of crime in itself.

I went home in a gloomy mood, despite all the Omega oil coursing through my veins. I told Celia I would think things over. I had trouble sleeping that night. I had nightmares. Too many thoughts and problems were dancing around in my head.

* * *

I couldn't help wondering why this conservatorship was so important. Zack had a little money, I suppose, and the cottage he lived in had to be worth something. Real estate prices are crazy in the Bay Area. Even after the bubble burst, as I said, it was if houses were made out of solid gold. But even so, his cottage was not the sort of property that attracted the real estate vultures. There was something going on here, but I had no idea what. Had somebody discovered oil, underneath the cottage? Did Zack own a rare postage stamp, from the Hawaiian Islands, without knowing it, something worth millions?

The very next day, believe it or not, the conservatorship cropped up again, from another source. I had a phone call, and then a visit, from Roger Greenhouse.

He was impeccably dressed and very lawyerlike. He wore a conservative tie, pale blue shirt and a dark suit. Even the gray at his temples looked suave and professional. I thought: three brothers, but so different. One was barely functioning; the second had been a drunk and a misfit and was also quite dead. And here was the third one, looking like a million dollars.

I said: "So sorry to hear about your loss."

He waved his hand, as if to dismiss this pious platitude, and said, "I've been told you're investigating my brother's death, is that correct?"

"What? Me? Investigating?"

"That's what I've heard. And it's not correct?"

"Absolutely not, Mr. Greenhouse."

"Roger."

"Absolutely not, Roger. I don't know where you could get such an idea. Yes, I've been representing Cynthia Greenhouse, Edgar's ex-wife; and I'm in touch with the members of her family, and, on certain matters, I've represented them too. But investigations? No way. I mean, I'm not a detective, I never do criminal work, so you see, whatever you heard, well, it just isn't correct."

"My brother was murdered. Somebody should be doing something about that," he said.

"Naturally," I said, "the police. I'm sure they're trying to get to the bottom of this. They take murder seriously."

"Oh, the police. They're totally incompetent. And they're on the outside, if you know what I mean. They don't know about family matters, and.... the dynamics of, well, personal relationships. Look: if you're not looking into the matter, could I tempt you to do some work on this? I know you're not a detective. But there are other aspects of the situation.... I've got money, I'm willing to pay. It's a question of ... family. You know. Brothers. I don't know if you have brothers and sisters. Edgar and I, we weren't close, the last few years; but still, he was my flesh and blood. And somebody killed him. I'd like to know why."

"I understand that. Naturally. But how could I help?"

"You've got a reputation, Frank. I know you're trying to be modest. But I've been told that in the past, well, you've cleared up some cases, serious cases. Cases where the police didn't have a clue. Not through orthodox detective work, I know that; but somehow, you succeeded where other people failed."

"Roger, I'm flattered, but no. If I cleared up some matters, it was sheer luck. Look: I do a lot of estates work, small businesses, general law practice; but I avoid anything criminal, or anything that anybody would call investigation. That's just not my life. There are a lot of good private detectives—"

It was as if he hadn't heard a word I said. "My brother Edgar," he went on, "I know he was in some kind of trouble. Things hadn't worked out for him, for some time. You know, the marriage was a disaster. Then he drank too much, he lost clients because of that; and he was deep in debt. I know because I lent him some money. I think he was involved in, well, certain other things, things that weren't exactly kosher. He and that woman, Melissa, they worked together, and they were having an affair, too. I don't know what they were up to. Maybe it had something to do with drugs, who knows. I just know it wasn't, well, ordinary legal work. Maybe they got in too deep. Maybe somebody decided to get rid of him, and paid or hired somebody to dispose of him. I just don't know."

"I hadn't seen him in years. I wouldn't know anything about it," I said.

"Of course not. I'm not saying you did. Only.... I thought you might be able to help. You know, the neighbors saw the killer—did you know that? It was dark, they couldn't identify him, but they saw this man leaving the house—in a tan jacket; and it was just about that time, I guess, that he was killed. So who was that man? If my theory is right, it was somebody that was hired, a hired gun. But I'd like to know who was behind it. And why."

I wondered how he would react, if he found that I could in fact identify the sinister figure seen leaving the house. Why was everybody so convinced that this man murdered Edgar Greenhouse? This shadowy figure could have been a salesman who knocked on the door, trying to hawk a vacuum cleaner. Or somebody from Jehovah's Witnesses, selling their magazine or whatever they do.

"Wish I could help," I said. "But you understand my position—"

"Well, I suppose I have to understand. I wish I knew more.... I can't get anything out of that broad, Melissa. She's tough as nails," he said. "I don't trust her as far as I can throw her; and given the way she's built, I couldn't throw her very far. Anyway, there is another matter, and here I don't think you'd object, and you could be very helpful."

"Yes?"

He said: "I've been going over his papers, Edgar's papers. His files, stuff in his office, trying to straighten everything out, and figure out what to do. He didn't have many clients these days, but there were some, and naturally, there's some loose ends. He had a couple of clients who were involved in a minor real estate deal; I won't bore you with the details, a duplex over in Cupertino. I can take that one over. This is the sort of thing I do in my own practice, so it won't be any problem. I think the clients will agree. But there was another matter, and I was wondering about it. You know, for many years, he had a family law practice. Most of it was gone, and, as far as I can tell, he had nothing going, no current divorce matters at all, but he did have one issue, involving a conservatorship—"

An alarm bell went off in my mind. "Really? A conservatorship? Could you, uh, tell me more about it?"

"Well, it's an old man, Zack Winters; he's a brother of Mose Winters. You know who I mean, Mose is Daisy Winters' father-in-law; and she's the sister of Edgar's ex-wife. But you know all that. Anyway, Zack Winters is very old and apparently he's losing it. That's a familiar story; but this case is a little, well, unconventional. The petitioner isn't a member of the family, it's a woman, Anna Petrovna, she's a Russian immigrant, and she's his housekeeper. There must be something here I don't quite get."

"She's actually filed a petition? The family has been talking about setting something up, but I didn't think anything had been done as yet."

"Oh yes, this Anna, she filed a petition, but there hasn't been any hearing, no court appearance, nothing settled or decided. The petition—I saw a copy—it alleges that Winters is mentally incompetent, and needs the services of a conservator; that he has no immediate family, except a brother who is himself very elderly. It goes on to say that the petitioner, Anna Petrovna, is a close personal friend, and has been informally managing his estate, and taking care of his personal needs. I don't know what this is all about. Maybe it's completely normal. When I asked this Melissa person about this, she refused to talk to me. Weird. I've never handled anything like this; I don't know much about this branch of the law, conservators, estates, guardians. I suppose it could get complicated."

"Definitely," I said. "And in this case, certainly."

"And you've have some experience with these things, conservatorships?"

"Actually, I have, but—"

"Good. Then I'd like you to take it over, now that Edgar's gone. I don't have any objection to this Anna person. Maybe she'd be a great conservator. But somebody has to handle the legal side of it. We can't just drop this. So, why not you. You know the family, after all; you can talk to them."

"I can't do this, Roger. There's a conflict of interest here. I can't represent this woman, this Anna person; remember, I represent Cynthia Greenhouse, and this is her brother-in-law's uncle. Clyde Winters' uncle. And the old brother, Mose, lives with all of them, shares a household. This much is absolutely certain: they would not want that woman taking over. They do not want her appointed anything. In fact, they would fight it tooth and nail."

"Really? Can you tell me why?"

"Because this woman.... I don't know this, I'm just repeating what I heard, but they say she's fleecing the estate, she's taking advantage of a sick old man; she's robbing him, she's exerting undue influence, and all the rest of it. The family wants her out of there, they want her fired; and they certainly don't want her legally empowered to run his affairs."

He frowned. "Did Edgar know this? About this ... rumor?"

"I have no idea."

"If it's true—and I'm not saying it is—maybe the best thing would be, just to forget about the matter; withdraw, I mean. I'm going to be executor of Edgar's estate. There's a will, too. He left everything to me. Everything—in a way, that's a bad joke. The estate is insolvent, as far as I can tell. Unless he has some hidden assets."

My mind flashed back to the scene in Edgar's cottage: the shabby furniture, the general state of disrepair. Hidden assets seemed unlikely.

"So, if I understand you, you'll just drop the conservatorship, you'll withdraw the petition?" I said, hopefully. Was it possible that Roger Greenhouse, of all people, would be able to rescue me from the clutches of Melissa Funk?

I certainly hoped so.

"Of course I can't do it on my own; I'll have to talk to this Anna person," he said. "After all, she's the petitioner. But yes, I might try to get her to call the whole thing off. Now that I know it would be contested, there wouldn't be any point to going on."

"We'd all be grateful to you," I said, "if you could get her to withdraw the petition."

That was the end of our conversation. I couldn't believe my good fortune. Roger Greenhouse as my savior. Life is full of tricks.

9

It was, at any rate, a light at the end of the tunnel—for me, anyway. A helpful development, something that could get me out of the clutches of Melissa Funk.

And yet the underlying mystery was thicker than ever. What was going on here? Everything seemed entangled in a funny way: an old man, teetering on the brink of senility, with a predatory housekeeper, who was, supposedly, taking advantage of him—and had the effrontery to file a petition to become his conservator. Why was this connected with Edgar's death? Or was it? And why would Edgar's death be connected to the death of some unnamed guy who was found dead in Lytton Park; and why should the unnamed guy be connected to the Greenhouse and Winters families, to Edgar's ex-wife, and her relatives? It just didn't add up.

And who was this woman, Anna Petrovna, anyway, and what was she up to? Granted, she was trying to fleece poor old Zack. Maybe this was a case of elder abuse, but it seemed as if something darker and more sinister was going on.

Naturally, I wanted the problems to go away. Roger was helping me out, without being aware of it. But I was, alas, not done with the conservatorship. Clyde came to see me, on behalf of Mose "and the rest of the family," to ask me for help. "This woman," he said, "she's actually filed a petition, she has the gall to think she should be named conservator. Imagine! Putting the fox in charge of the hen house. We'll fight it, of course."

He wanted to know what steps I would take. I told him that I had had a conversation with Roger Greenhouse, that he was handling Edgar's affairs, that this conservatorship was something Edgar had been handling, but that he, Roger, had decided to call the whole thing off.

"Frank, that's great," he said. "You're a wonder. How did you do it?"

I didn't have the heart to tell him that Roger's decision had little or nothing to do with my lawyerly skills. I just smiled.

"Can we be sure he'll follow through?" Clyde asked.

"Well, no, we can't be sure; but don't worry, I'll keep an eye on things," I said.

"Oh, that would be great. And look: just to make sure, can't we do something on our own? Mose is willing to act, he's the closest relative.... Zack has nobody else, at least nobody else that lives within thousands of miles."

I promised to take a look at the file, and see whether the petition had been withdrawn. I found time to go to the courthouse, and after dealing with the usual surly and incompetent clerk, a woman with pimples who seemed to resent being asked to do anything at all, I was able to read the petition and look at the file. To my surprise, among the papers was a formal objection to the petition, not from the family, which had been, until recently, unaware of the petition—but from Sandra Saunders, of all people. How on earth did she get involved?

I decided to call on Sandra and talk to her about this matter. Zack's problems were, after all, legitimately part of my job. On my lunch hour, I drove to the Stanford campus. I parked near the Faculty Club, paid the parking fee, and walked on campus to the office where she was working. It was located in what is called the Inner Quad, which is the oldest part of the campus, and by far the most beautiful. It consists of a gigantic set of interlocking squares, with vast courtyards in between, lined with quiet loggias. Students in their jeans and flip-flops sprawled in the courtyard, eating lunch. I found Sandra's office easily. She was sitting at her desk, eating Bulgarian yogurt.

"Hi Sandra," I said. She looked up. She obviously did not recognize me. I reminded her who I was, and told her I was working for the Winters family.

"Yeah? So what?"

"Well, it's that petition—the one you filed, with regard to Zack Winters. Can you tell me what's this all about?"

. "It's none of your business."

"Sorry, but it is very much my business. I told you, I'm representing the Winters family; Zack's brother Mose, he's very much concerned...."

"Oh, is he? The hell he is. He doesn't give a crap."

"You're wrong there," I said. "He cares a lot."

"Yeah? Well, if he cared, they wouldn't be trying to do this to Zack."

"They're not trying to do anything to him, only take care of him."

"Really," she said, her voice dripping with sarcasm. "Then why don't they leave him alone? Why are they trying to railroad him?"

It dawned on me that she thought *we* had been behind the petition, that *we* were the ones trying to put Zack into conservatorship. Well, that was true; but not the way she imagined, and certainly not for the reasons she imagined.

I told her we had nothing to do with Anna's petition and were prepared to fight it ourselves; and what was Sandra's role in this matter anyway?

"Look, Mr. Lawyer, I just don't like injustice. Of any kind. Couple three years ago, I met Zack. He was one of the people in my study. I work on memory, old people's memory. I get really thick with some of my subjects. It's not exactly in the protocol, there's all this bullshit about pure science, but I don't believe there is such a thing. Pure science. That's just something dreamed up by white, hegemonic men."

I couldn't help pointing out that Zack was himself a white, hegemonic man.

"He's white, but he's not hegemonic. He's pathetic, that's what he is. You know, if you live long enough, and if you start losing your grip, then, I tell you, you might as well be black, you're an honorary African-American, if you know what I mean. You're cheated and robbed and treated like dirt. I used to go see him once in a while; and to tell you the truth, I didn't like the set-up, this woman he had there lately, she was like some kind of Nazi, ordering him around. And he told me a bunch of stuff, how people were out to get him.... OK, he was slipping; and I could see this wasn't going in the right direction. Then he told me something about a petition, he wasn't clear about it, he didn't understand it; and I went to the courthouse and checked, and I saw, this bitch was trying to get control over him. So I thought it was time to put in my own two cents. I made up my mind to stop her."

"And you didn't talk to the family?"

"No, Mr. Lawyer, I didn't talk to your *clients*," she said, with a sneer. "What did they ever do for the guy? I figured, they were part of the whole vicious plot."

I tried to explain, patiently, that the family was not part of any plot, that they cared about Zack, cared deeply. And that Anna's petition actually caught them totally off balance. She said: "Oh yeah, then how come Edgar Greenhouse was involved? Remember, I knew him.... Isn't he the husband of your client? Well, he drafted the damn thing, you don't think this Anna person could do it on her own, when she barely speaks English?"

Again, I patiently explained that Edgar Greenhouse was Cynthia's ex-husband, not her husband; that in fact they didn't get along; and that, by the way, Edgar Greenhouse was extremely dead, murdered in fact. That news shut her up at least momentarily. She didn't seem to know he was dead. Unless she was acting. Maybe she killed him. Maybe she went around killing white, hegemonic men. I told her the family would do whatever it could to block the petition, and I thanked her for her concern. At that point, I felt I might as well leave, and I did.

* * *

I reported my news back to Clyde, and to Cynthia, and through them to Mose. They thanked me for my efforts. I left out a few salient facts, of course. I hoped that the petition would soon be withdrawn, thanks to Roger's efforts, and that I wouldn't have to lift a finger myself.

About a week later, I went to the courthouse and I checked

the file. The petition had indeed been withdrawn, and the whole issue was in abeyance. I felt as if a stone had been lifted off my chest.

I should have felt even better after a phone call from Melissa Funk, which came the next day. She sounded quite strange, but what she told me was welcome news. She said the petition had been withdrawn, and that was good. She also told me, that I should forget our conversation; she had said dumb things to me, but not to pay any attention. She said she was sure now, that I didn't kill Edgar Greenhouse ("Gee, thanks," I said). She said, she had no intention of going to the police, and she was washing her hands of the whole affair.

"Forget anything I said," she said again. "As far as I'm concerned the whole thing is over. Zack and Anna. Everything."

I thanked her for the news and hung up. It was indeed good news, but her tone of voice was odd, even alarming. This was a phone conversation, so I couldn't see her face, but she sounded upset, agitated, worried—maybe even frightened. And she raised as many questions as she answered. I'm glad she realized I didn't kill Edgar Greenhouse. But what led her to that realization? Who had she been talking to? Roger Greenhouse? Anna?

Was it possible that she knew I was innocent, because she knew somebody else was guilty? And if so, who?

* * *

The days went by. It seemed obvious, from the thick silence, that the police were getting nowhere, with regard to both cases. Nowhere on the death in Lytton Park, and nowhere on the murder of Edgar Greenhouse. Every day I looked at the local throwaway newspaper. I skimmed over news about sewer bonds and broken street lights, ads for nannies and the sale of old pianos. But there was never anything about either murder. It was all very unsettling. Now that I was no longer frightened of Melissa Funk, I felt my old vice, curiosity, creeping over me, burrowing deep into my skin.

But it was more than curiosity. *Somebody* had killed those two men. It could have been armed robbers, or total strangers;

but that seemed too much to swallow. I had this gnawing feeling, in the pit of my stomach, that it was somebody I knew: that somebody I had met, talked to, maybe even discussed the case with, had brutally murdered two men. And behind that somebody was some dark and furtive motive. There was no obvious *reason* to kill the two men; but nobody kills without a reason—well, almost nobody. And I didn't see any signs of a serial killer, a raving psychopath on the horizon. What, then, was to be done?

10

What was to be done? The smart answer was: nothing. Stay out of it. I could almost hear Celia's voice in my ear, warning, admonishing, filling my brain with good advice that I was completely incapable of following.

So, contrary to this (unheard but felt) advice, I decided to do something. I decided to speak to that woman, Anna Petrovna. She seemed to be in some sense the key to the mystery. And I knew where I could find her. After all, she was living in Zack's place, in some spare room or other.

It was time, then, to pay a visit to the old man. I gave the family the good news about the petition; I said I thought I'd like to visit Zack, get some idea of the lay of the land.

"That's a great idea," Cynthia said. "I can't thank you enough."

I got his phone number from Mose, and I called, but there was absolutely no answer: the phone rang and rang, and nothing happened. No message, no answering machine, no voice mail. I knew Zack was home—where else would he be? It didn't surprise me that he had not joined the modern world. Today, we expect an answering machine, or voice mail, or the like. Everybody I know has something along these lines. In some ways, it's one of the great inventions of recent years. It ranks with the cell phone and cash machines, jet airplanes and air conditioning. It's right up there.

Take my mother, for example: she used to complain all the time that I never called her. I would say, yes, mother, I called, but nobody answered; you must have been out. Of course, she thought I was lying. She would say, "Out? Where do I go? I never go out." In fact, she did go out. She went to the Safeway for groceries, and she played bridge with her neighbors. "I did call, mother, honestly I did."

But now I have proof. My sister and I made sure she had some kind of voicemail. If I play my cards right, I call when she's off playing bridge, or shopping at the Safeway, or sitting at the senior center, comparing notes with other old ladies. Half of them are talking about how rotten their children are, how they never call, how they pay no attention, how selfish they are, or they complain about sons-in-law and daughters-in-law, two groups that are apparently inherently rotten; and half of them (conversely) go on about how wonderful their children are, how caring, how much attention they shower on their old mother, even though they're so busy after winning the Nobel Prize in medicine, or an election to the Senate, or completing a rare heart transplant; sometimes it's the same mothers only at different times. Anyway, now I can leave a message, "Hi Mom, I called, but you weren't in."

I have to confess: I always hated calling my mother, because of her constant litany of complaints. Complaints about me, about my sister, and about arthritis, her sciatic nerve, about the landlord—in short, about everything. And complaints about the neighbors, and the young couple who moved in upstairs and play their radio so loud at night. Do all old ladies complain so much? I hope not. Leaving a message helps. If, of course, she remembers to check for her messages. Sometimes she does.

* * *

Zack, of course, had nothing but a land line. No cell phone. Alas, he was passing up another great invention. The cell phone has so many uses. And it's a real time-saver. I've made countless calls while shopping, driving (this is forbidden, but I do it anyway), and even while urinating. You can use the cell phone anywhere, anytime, and while you're doing almost anything, with the possible exception of sexual intercourse. And who knows? Maybe some people have figured out a way to do that too. They might find it a special thrill.

I was walking from the office to my car, and I whipped out my cell phone and called Cynthia. I said, I thought I ought to talk to Zack on the phone, before I dropped in on him; but I had called and called, and there was no answer, and did she know what that was all about?

"It's strange. Usually that woman answers."

"Well, nobody answered."

"Mose has a key. I can borrow it. Maybe we should go there together, and see for ourselves."

This was on a Friday afternoon; Cynthia suggested Saturday morning. I drove to Cynthia's house and picked her up. She tried once more to reach Zack on her cell phone. There was no answer.

"I hope there's nothing wrong," she said.

Zack lived in a tiny cottage in Menlo Park. The layout reminded me of Edgar's arrangements. The cottage, which looked for all the world like a remodeled garage, stood off to the left of a big rambling two-story house. The main house sat on a plot of land which was fairly large, as urban lot-sizes go. The cottage had obviously seen better days. It needed a paint job badly. Once there had been vines growing on the sides, no doubt producing beautiful flowers; something had obviously blighted the vines, and all that was left was a collection of naked twigs and branches. The windows were caked with dust and grime. If Anna was supposed to be a housekeeper, she had done very little keeping of house.

We rang a rusty door bell. No answer. We tried several times. We followed a little gravel path around the side of the house, and looked in the only window where the shades weren't drawn.

We saw Zack. He was sitting on a sofa, with his head down—apparently dozing off. The television set was on. We could see the flashing images on the screen. His walker was next to the sofa.

We pounded on the window. No response. "He's a bit deaf," Cynthia said. We pounded louder. Either he heard us, or he woke up spontaneously, and happened to turn his head and see us. Cynthia signaled to him, as best she could, to let us in.

It took him a while to pull himself laboriously off the sofa, get the walker, and drag his creaking old bones to the door; it took what seemed like fifteen minutes or more before he actually got it open. From the sound effects, it seemed clear to me that he had bolts and locks and locks and bolts.

Cynthia gave him a hug, which he more or less ignored. He stared at me, and said, "Who's this?" Cynthia introduced me, and gave a brief explanation. Zack grunted. Actually, we had met before, and probably more than once. But I was obviously not memorable enough to establish myself in the aging hard drive of his brain.

We went back into the sitting-room. There was a musty odor in the house. The furniture was better than Edgar's, but the floor clearly needed a good mopping. He sat down on the sofa, and briefly closed his eyes. I was afraid he would fall asleep again.

"Zack," Cynthia said, in a loud voice. "Zack, listen to us. We have to talk to you, OK? Where's Anna?"

"How the hell should I know? Damn woman. She just up and left. I was taking a nap, and I said to her, you wake me up, don't leave me sleep all day, I got this program I want to watch. I like to watch this program, Judge Marcie, she comes on after lunch, she's a real judge, you know? The jerks that come on the program, you wouldn't believe; but Judge Marcie, she knows her stuff, she doesn't take any guff, and she really gives it to them, well, I forget to watch it sometimes, but I don't like missing it. That's why I said, Anna, don't let me oversleep. But I did oversleep. When I finally woke up, I called her, I said, get your butt in here, I'd like something to eat, and why didn't you wake me? Well, naturally she didn't answer, seeing as how she was gone. She just wasn't here."

"When was this?"

"Was it yesterday? I don't know. I thought she'd come back. Not that I wanted her. Big dumb bitch. I'm glad to be rid of her. But I didn't get any supper. She used to cook stuff for me, or have something delivered. Her own cooking, I hated it. Always tasted lousy, she put in too much salt. I got so hungry I could eat a shoe. I found a box of crackers in the pantry. You know, it's hard for me to get around. I been eating the crackers. Where the hell is that woman?"

"Why didn't you call your brother? Or call me?"

"I thought, she's gonna come back. I mean, I'm paying her good money. They say she's stealing my money. I don't know. I get confused."

"Your brother's worried about you," she said.

"Yeah, that'll be the day. Fat lot he cares." Then he turned to me and gave me a blank stare. He turned to Cynthia, and said "Who the hell is this?"

She said, "I told you, Zack. This is Frank May. He's my lawyer. . He's, well, the family lawyer. We'd like to help you out."

"A lawyer? What for? What kind of help? I don't need help. And I don't need lawyers. Bunch of bloodsuckers. I never met a good one in my life."

I swallowed my pride. Cynthia went on, in a gentle tone of voice. "Well, uncle Zack, there's some good ones; and Frank here, he's one of the good ones. The fact is, we're really worried about you. Your situation...."

"What about it? Hey, I'm hungry. I can't live on a box of crackers. Cynthia, can you get me something to eat?"

"Of course. But first, can we talk for a little bit?"

"How about first getting me something to eat. Man, I'm starving."

"Suppose we took you out, took you to a restaurant; how would you like that?"

He shook his head no. "I'm not up to it. Too hard. I can't get in and out of cars, it's not easy for me. Anyway, she doesn't want me to go out. That woman."

Cynthia said: "She's not here, Zack."

"Well, she'll come back."

He closed his eyes, and seemed to be dozing off again. Cynthia went into the kitchen, and I followed her. The place was disgusting.. Dirty dishes were piled up in the sink. She opened the refrigerator. There was an awful rancid smell.

Cynthia took out a container of cottage cheese, and opened it. The insides were green with mold. She threw it into a garbage can.

She went into the pantry and found a can of vegetable soup. She took steel wool, and attacked one of the pots—all of them were in the sink, caked with crud—and got it relatively clean. Then she rinsed it, boiled some water and poured it in the pot, wiped the pot, and heated up the soup. Zack was snoring in the other room. She washed a bowl and a spoon, poured the soup into it, and woke up Zack. He wolfed down the soup, spilling some of it on his shirt, which was wrinkled and dirty enough to begin with. Cynthia handed him a napkin.

"We've got to get somebody in here to take care of him," she said.

"I don't want anybody," he said. "I can take care of myself. Maybe just somebody to make me something to eat. I like it when somebody cooks. The rest, I can do. I got my walker. I go to the bathroom OK."

Cynthia said: "Zack, I know you can manage. But why should you? We can get somebody, somebody good, it'll make things easier, she'll cook for you, but she'll also clean the place up, help you with things you need. How does that sound? And maybe take you out someplace, get you some air, you're cooped up in here, you're like a prisoner."

"I *am* a prisoner."

"No, no, you're not. What a crazy idea."

"I'm her prisoner. That big dumb broad. She scares me. People want to kill me, I know it. She's part of it."

"Nobody's trying to kill you, Zack."

"They're trying, all right. I don't know who exactly. Maybe the mafia. That Russian woman, she was with the mafia. I didn't know it at the time. I thought she was going to kill me. I think she was putting pieces of glass in the food. I wouldn't touch it, unless she ate some of it first; then I could eat it. I just know they want to kill me."

"Listen, Zack, I told you," she said, "Nobody wants to kill you. Honestly, Zack."

"Yeah? How about that guy, the one in the park. They

killed him alright. I was gonna be next. That's why he had that address and phone number, it was on a piece of paper; Mose told me about it.

"But it wasn't your address and phone number, Zack."

"Well, it was my brother's.... Maybe he's in on it, you think I trust him? Hell, no. He's my closest relative in this country—maybe he'd get all my money if something happened to me."

"Your own brother? He wouldn't take your money, Zack."

"Oh wouldn't he? He always loved money, the old goat. And when Fanny died, I changed my will, I left some of the money to Mose, and I told him about it, that was my big mistake."

"Well, why don't you change your will again, Zack, if you're not happy. Frank here, he could handle it."

"Change it? Why? I don't have anybody else. I could leave it to you, Cynthia."

"I don't need it, Zack. Your daughters...."

"Daughters? I've got daughters? Where the hell are they? They live someplace, I don't know where. It's hard to remember sometimes. I don't owe them a thing. They never come by. Anyway, how do I even know they were mine? You think I trusted Fanny?"

"Well," she said, "you could leave money to charity."

"What kind of charity? Nobody ever gave me any charity, so why should I give it to somebody else. I don't want anybody to get my money. I don't know how much I have.... It's in the bank. Can't remember which one. Also, I get social security. A bunch of checks come in the mail. Anna, she signs them, I think. I don't know what she does with the money. She wanted me to sign something, she said, power of attorney, I didn't sign it, and she got furious, she doesn't like it when I don't do what she wants; she was as red as a beet, and she was cursing me, in Russian. I think it was Russian. Tell you the truth, I been scared of her. She was big as an ox—did you ever see her? I think she could kill me, like that, if she wanted to do. She said to me, you're old, and sick, and worthless. But what could I do?"

Cynthia said: "Zack: why didn't you call me?"

He said: "She was always watching. The phone. I wanted to wait till she left the house. But she pulled out the plugs when she went away. I said to Edgar...."

"Edgar?"

"Yeah. Edgar. He came here sometimes. I said to him, I don't like her, can't you get rid of her; but he just laughed and said, it's gonna be all right. But it wasn't. I thought she was going to kill me. I said to myself, maybe I better get to her first. I've got a gun, did you know that? I mean, I had a gun. I thought, if she tries anything, I'll shoot her. I kept it in a drawer. It was locked. You're supposed to lock up a gun. They told me that."

Cynthia said: "You never told me about the gun, Zack. I don't like guns. You shouldn't have a gun around."

He said: "It's not there. It's gone. She took it. She was asleep, I got up, got my walker, and I went to the drawer. I told you, it was supposed to be locked. Anyway, it wasn't. I don't know where the key is, tell you the truth. I lost it, I think. I opened the drawer, and the gun wasn't there. I tell you, she took it."

Cynthia said: "Show me the drawer, Zack."

"It's right in there, in my bedroom. The dresser. Top drawer. Just take a look. But it's not there. I told you that; she took it with her. Maybe she's gonna hold up a bank."

Cynthia and I went into the bedroom. This was as big a mess as the rest of the house. Nobody had made the bed in days; at any rate, that's the way it looked. Dirty clothes lay on the floor in heaps: shirts, socks, underwear. To the left of the bed, there was a dresser, with three drawers. We opened the top drawer, and, to our surprise, a gun *was* there. "My God," Cynthia said.

She took the gun out of the drawer, and we went back into the living room. "Zack," she said, "the gun was right there. In the drawer."

He looked puzzled. "I could have sworn it wasn't. Maybe it was there all the time. My memory, it isn't what it used to be, I get confused sometimes.... Maybe she took it, that Anna, and then she brought it back later."

"Why would she do that?"

"How the hell should I know? She does what she damn pleases. God, I hope she doesn't come back. I hated her. But somebody's got to get me my food."

Cynthia took me aside, and asked me, what we should do about the gun. I said we certainly weren't going to leave the gun here in Zack's house. And I wondered: was he right, when he said the gun had been missing? True, his memory was as full of holes as a Swiss cheese, but still, he could be right. I had a horrible thought: maybe Anna took the gun, maybe she went out, and shot Edgar with it. But why would she bring it back? Why not just throw it in the Bay? It seemed stupid to replace it. Senseless.

Still, people often do stupid things.

We talked about the situation, and we decided to turn the gun over to the police. Zack certainly hadn't used it. If anybody was going to be in trouble, it would be this Anna person; and we had no reason to try to protect her. Most likely the gun had been sitting there all the time, but this was a lead worth pursuing. There was some connection here with Edgar; so the gun was, or could be, relevant. Cynthia volunteered to take the gun to the police, and I was happy to let her do it.

She had another task, too: finding somebody to take care of Zack. Clearly, he needed help. Cynthia had been using the word "she," but Zack was stubborn. This time he wanted a man. "I've had enough of these women, they just boss you around."

The next few days, Cynthia and Daisy took turns making Zack his meals, and they hired a cleaning service to come in and do a job on the house. Cynthia also managed to find someone more or less permanent, through an agency called Household Helpers, Inc. This was a bright and eager young man from the Philippines, a trained nurse, studying to get certified in California. He worked out perfectly. He was efficient and caring, and a stickler for cleanliness. Zack was not the easiest of patients. He grumbled at first about the food, "all that foreign stuff. I like plain food, not anything weird." But Vic knew exactly how to adjust to people like Zack. Meanwhile, Cynthia took over Zack's finances; she paid bills, deposited checks, and got his affairs in better order.

The family dropped the whole idea of a conservatorship, at least for the time being. Between Victor, the caregiver, and Cynthia, Zack was well cared for. On Victor's days off, his agency sent a substitute. Zack kept on grumbling about everything, but in fact he seemed rather pleased. I drafted a power of attorney, in favor of Cynthia, and although Zack was reluctant, we were patient and persistent, and in the end he signed it.

Anna never came back. She had obviously packed up her few belongings, because there was nothing left of hers in the cottage—nothing even to remind us she had been there. Been there and in fact had been very much in charge. Now she was simply gone.

11

The arrangements for Zack took time, of course. Meanwhile, there was progress of sorts in the two murder cases. I heard the news from Cynthia. She called me at the office, very excited, even agitated.

"Cynthia, what's wrong? You sound... well, disturbed."

"Frank, I am disturbed. You won't believe this. I just got done talking to two detectives, I thought they'd never go, they asked me so many questions ... all about the gun...."

"What about it?"

"They say it's the murder weapon. They did tests or whatever they do, and they say it's absolutely sure. It's the one."

"The murder weapon? You mean, it's the gun that killed Edgar?"

"Yes. But not only Edgar, Frank. That's the amazing part. They say it's the gun that killed the man in the park. They still don't know who he is, but.... Frank, I'm scared. What's going on here? Who's killing these people, and why? And who *was* that man? The one in the park? How was he connected to us? And to Edgar?"

"I don't know," I said. "But it has something to do with that woman—Anna."

"Why, Frank? Who is she? What does she want? I told the police all about her, and how she took the gun from the drawer—it had to be her, no? But I don't know if they'll find her. She's gone. Frank, do you think she's the one? Do you think she killed Edgar?"

"Well, maybe," I said. "She had the gun. We know Edgar knew this other guy, the guy in Lytton Park; maybe he was a client. And this Anna, she was connected to Edgar, somehow...."

"But where did she come from? Who hired her in the first place?"

"Cynthia, it was Edgar that hired her. But ... I can't imagine he did it on his own. He must have consulted somebody in your family."

"Not me."

"Well, then, maybe Daisy; or Clyde, or Claude. Or maybe Mose himself. I know you're a close-knit family, but still. To hire somebody like that, it would be the right thing to do, I mean, to ask the family, Zack's nephews, his brother. It's only logical."

"I don't think any of us were involved. I really don't. It's ... not the way we are." But then she paused. She saw the point—and it disturbed her. She said, ruefully: "Maybe you're right. But I hope not. The family.... Do you think? Oh no—it couldn't be."

"Stranger things have happened, Cynthia."

She was silent again. Then she said: "Do you want me to try to find out? Find out if one of us, well, had something to do with this Anna?"

"Please, Cynthia."

But she called me the next day, and said she talked to both Clyde and Claude; and to Mose, too, and to Daisy; and none of them claimed they had given Edgar the go-ahead. Had Edgar acted on his own? If so, why? And who gave him the authority? Nobody, apparently.

Except Clyde, in a way. He had said he had nothing at all to do with it. Cynthia said to him, "But somebody did. Zack didn't come up with the idea. He's not that organized, and he wouldn't have gone to Edgar, by himself." Then Clyde told her (according to Cynthia) that in a way he felt somewhat responsible. "You'll be surprised, Frank. Clyde told me, he remembered, he had been worried about the situation, and he happened to mention it to Edgar."

"Edgar? Cynthia, why on earth would he do that?"

"I honestly don't know. Clyde said he bumped into Edgar, had lunch with him. I didn't know they were friendly, and frankly, I don't like it. But anyway. Somehow the subject came up, you know, about Zack, and his problems. Clyde said the old man was losing it, and something should be done. And Edgar volunteered to help out, he said he knew somebody, an immigrant woman, and she'd be perfect for the job, and just leave it to him. And Clyde said he was happy to have the matter off his hands."

Something about the story sounded fishy to me, Clyde forgetting and suddenly remembering. But I had nothing concrete to go on. Why Cynthia's ex-husband should involve himself in this affair was a mystery. I told Cynthia I thought something sounded odd, and she agreed. "Believe me, it's not like Edgar to do a good deed. I know I'm an ex-wife, and ex-wives are bitter people, but you have to trust me on this. The milk of human kindness long ago turned sour with Edgar. Really."

I had an awful thought. The woman was supposedly stealing money from Zack, emptying his bank accounts, and so on. Suppose it was part of a plot; suppose Edgar had hired her to do that, and was going to share in these ill-gotten gains. We know Edgar had serious money problems.

But how much loot was there? Zack had a bit of income; he had monthly pension checks and Social Security checks, and he owned his little place. I suppose he had some money in the bank and some securities. I could imagine a greedy housekeeper helping herself to some of the money, but did it merit a whole conspiracy? Involving Edgar? It really seemed like small potatoes.

And why would she kill Edgar? If she did. Clearly, Anna had to be the number one suspect at this time. I told Cynthia that the police would be looking for her, and they'd find her in due course. That might very well be the end of the matter, and a good thing too. As I thought about it, it seemed to me extremely likely that she was the one. After all, she had access to the gun. Zack was muddled, to be sure, and his short-term memory was exceedingly porous. Still, I believed him when he said the gun had been missing at one point, maybe two points. Somebody took it and used it as a murder weapon. We have no idea *why* Anna would want to kill Edgar, and the mysterious other guy, too, the guy in Lytton Park. But presumably that would come out eventually.

I was sitting in my office, thinking about all of these things, and trying to avoid work. I had to draft a trust agreement for one of my clients, another grumpy old man, Vittorio, a cousin of Joe Zingarelli. Vittorio, like his cousin, had been in the restaurant business. He had owned an Italian restaurant, in San Carlos, and it was wildly successful. But Vittorio was older than Joe, he was tired of running the restaurant—it was backbreaking work—and he had nobody to take it over. Anyway, Vittorio sold his restaurant to three Latvian immigrants, who had money from God knows where, and they promptly ran the restaurant into bankruptcy. I suppose they had no feel for Italian food, and nobody wanted Latvian food, whatever that might be.

Vittorio, however, came out very well. He had insisted on cash, and they paid him tons of it. He put the money into Treasury bills, resisting the temptations of the stock market. As a result, he was currently sitting pretty. The trust, however, was highly complex. That's because his life was highly complex: three ex-wives, and a whole slew of legitimate and illegitimate children, ranging in age from seven to thirty-seven, and, except for the seven year old, he was either quarreling with them or getting over a quarrel with them. He kept changing his mind about which ones he considered the biggest ingrates, and which ones actually deserved to get some of his money. For a while, he was particularly venomous toward his third oldest son, Stefano, who was gay, and had the temerity to come to a family dinner, on Thanksgiving no less, with a boyfriend, who was not only gay but Chinese.

"Vittorio," I said, "I know Stefano, he's a good boy, try to understand, OK?" But it was no use at all. Stefano was effectively disinherited. But then Stefano was eclipsed by his sister Benedetta, the oldest daughter, who smoked, ran through two husbands in two years, wore mini-skirts, and called her father an "asshole" to his face. There were other sons, but they were all terrible disappointments. "Luke, he's a drummer in some God-awful band, the shit they call music nowadays.... I told him, I didn't want to listen to that crap, and anyway he won't make a dime, believe me, and the life they lead, it's disgusting. Up all night with and nothing but fucking around and then they sleep until noon. Where did I go wrong? And Vincent, he's a lazy bum, dropped out of college, and he smokes pot and screws around; I'm fed up with him." All of these ins and outs and family turmoils led to endless drafting and re-drafting of documents, as Vittorio kept changing his mind. The latest complication was Vittorio's plan to get married again. Wife number four was a former waitress in his restaurant, some thirty years younger than Vittorio, and pregnant with what was apparently his child.

I was also involved in drafting a letter to a client, on an extremely involved custody issue. As I think I mentioned be-fore. I had spent countless hours on this problem. I like doing wills and trusts, and handling estates. I don't like the rest of family law, especially divorce and custody. I don't like confront-ing the raw, naked hatred that these issues seem to evoke.

But all this is neither here nor there. For the most part. The custody case was actually important, actually a help; but I'll tell you about that somewhat later. At this point, in the midst of a daydream, which had interrupted my draftsmanship, I had a phone call from Melissa Funk, close to the last person in the world I wanted to hear from, demanding to see me. I said I was busy that afternoon.

"Busy with what? You don't have ten minutes to spare?"

In some ways, I'm weak and easily buffaloed; I caved in and agreed to see her. She arrived on time, garishly dressed, as I expected, wearing a skirt much too short for a woman of her age. She was slightly disheveled. Her dyed orange hair needed touching up. The gray was beginning to show.

I was frankly nervous about this visit. The conservatorship issue had gone away; Anna's petition was withdrawn, and Anna herself was out of the picture. This was all to the good. But Melissa had no reason now to protect me from the police. I half-expected her to announce she was going to turn me in, that she was going to tell the authorities big news—that she could actually identify for them the mysterious, skulking figure.

After a few perfunctory words, I said: "You know, I suppose, that the petition was withdrawn. The conservator thing. It's dead. You got what you wanted."

She said. "You had nothing to do with it."

"So what? I was going to take some steps. I was. Now I don't have to. How it happened, doesn't matter. In a way, you owe me."

"I don't owe you anything," she said. "Don't give me that bull. I said I wouldn't go to the police ... but that was then. Now things are different."

A cold chill ran up my spine. "What good would it do you, Melissa? Think about it. What do you have to gain, telling the police some story."

"Why not, Frank? It's no story. It's the gospel truth."

I was speechless.

She gave a hoarse little laugh. She could read me like a book. She was clearly enjoying my misery. For a minute, that is. Then she said: "You don't have to worry. I'm not going to say boo. What kind of a heartless bitch do you think I am? I could screw up your life, but why should I? I never wanted to go to the police in the first place. The less I have to do with them the better. Besides, I know something now I didn't know before."

"You know something? What something?"

"I know you didn't kill Edgar. I told you that already. Actually, I never really thought you did it. You don't strike me as a murderer. Frankly, you haven't got the guts."

"Under the circumstances," I said, "I consider that a compliment."

"But that's not the main reason," she said. "I found out, you weren't the only one prowling around Edgar's house. I mean, somebody got there ahead of you. I think you were telling the truth. When you got there, he was already dead."

"I told you that myself," I said. "At least now you believe me. But who was it? Who was that somebody? And how did you find out?"

"Sorry. I'm not going to tell you. Not now, and not ever."

"Come on," I said, "I need to know. Was it a man? Or was it Anna?"

"Anna?" she said, with genuine surprise in her voice. "You really think it was Anna? My God you're a dope!" And she laughed out loud. "That's the stupidest thing I've heard in a long time. Anyway, she's gone. Did you know that?"

"Well," I said, "I did. I went to see Zack, along with Cynthia Greenhouse. The woman wasn't there. She hadn't been there for a day or two. And she took all her things."

"She's never coming back," Melissa said. "She ran away, as fast as her legs could carry her. And do you know why?"

"Not a clue."

"Because she's scared, you fool. Scared witless and shitless. She was scared to death. Let's put it this way: two people are dead already, and she was in line to be number three."

"Number three? But why?"

"You honestly don't know?"

"I honestly don't know."

"You think I'm going to tell you? I'd be the biggest fool on God's earth. Anna ... let's say she had good reason to go. Whoever killed Edgar would be bound to get to her—that's what she was afraid of. Get to her, the way they got to Vladimir."

"Vladimir? Who on earth is that?"

Melissa stopped cold. She had that tell-tale look on her face: the look that told me, she knew she had said too much. She snapped at me, "Never mind."

But it was too late. I knew. The dead man in Lytton Park—his name was Vladimir. At least now I knew *something*. I had part of a name. And more than just a name. Anybody I suppose can be named Vladimir; but the chances are pretty high that somebody named Vladimir was Russian. Russian—like Anna Petrovna. Two Russians. That couldn't be just a coincidence. Joe Zingarelli said, the man had an accent. And it was something like Polish. It was all beginning to fit together.

But what on earth did Russians have to do with all this? How did Edgar get involved with Russians? And Cynthia and her family? I had visions of shadowy, Russian figures, members of the mafia, big beefy ruthless men, standing outside the Kremlin, hip-deep in snow, wearing sinister fur hats and bulky coats; and hatching plots to monopolize the sale of natural gas to Baluchistan or whatever. But this was not the Kremlin, it was sunny California. That a man named Vladimir, and a woman named Anna Petrovna, suddenly appeared on the scene seemed to be, like all things Russian, a puzzle inside a riddle inside an enigma.

And what did Melissa Funk really want from me? Had she really come to tell me she was letting me off the hook? Or did she come to find out what, if anything, I knew about this mysterious Slavic plot? And of course I knew nothing. If she did not know this before, she must have realized it, when blurting out "Vladimir" took me by surprise. After that, she basically fell silent. It was, in fact, the end of our meeting. She said she had things to do, and she simply got up and left.

Right away, I picked up the phone and called Cynthia. She wasn't in, which I should have known—she had a job after all. I didn't want to disturb her at the office, so I left a message on her home phone. She must have checked the messages, because she called me back, later on in the afternoon. I told her I had news for her.

"News, Frank? Good or bad."

"Well, I think good. We're making some progress at last. I know the name—well, at least the first name—of the dead guy, the one in Lytton Park."

"You do? Who told you?"

"Melissa Funk, of all people. Edgar's associate or assistant or whatever she was."

"How did she know his name?"

"Well, frankly, Cynthia, I have no idea. And it kind-of slipped out of her. She didn't want to tell me, really. Anyway, this is interesting: he was probably a Russian. Same as this Anna woman. There might be a connection. And his name was Vladimir."

There was a strange silence at the other end. I said: "Cynthia? Are you there?"

She said, "yes," but in an odd, husky voice. "You said: Vladimir...?"

"Yes, Vladimir; his name was Vladimir. Why? You sound funny. Do you know him, Cynthia? You said you didn't."

She seemed to hesitate. Then she said: "Yes, I said so; and it's true, I didn't know him. But ... listen, Frank, we have to talk. Can you come over? I can't go out of the house right now, I left the office early, because Daisy had to go to the doctor, and I told her I would come and baby-sit little Clyde. There's nobody else here, except Mose, and he's upstairs watching TV or napping, or whatever. Please come, Frank. I really need to talk."

I would have liked to jump into my car and go straight to her house, but as luck would have it, I had clients coming in. I told Cynthia I would come by, but it would have to be somewhat later. It was 5:30 when I was finally able to clear my desk and leave. I drove straight over to Cynthia's house.

Daisy was still out, apparently. Cynthia was in the living room; little Clyde was on the floor, on a rug. They had been playing Chutes and Ladders. "Clyde, honey," she said to him, "I have to talk to this nice man. We'll finish the game later."

"No, now," the kid said, in an angry voice; and when Cynthia persisted, he began to scream and kick his feet. Kids can be difficult, of course; but this brat seemed especially so. Probably spoiled rotten. An only child of parents who had desperately wanted a child. Cynthia said: "Clyde, honey, do stop screaming. What will this nice man think?"

Clyde Jr. made it very clear how little he cared about the nice man, by coming over and kicking me in the shins, as hard as he could, which was pretty darn hard. I smiled and tried to ignore him. Cynthia scolded him, then she gave up, and asked me if I could wait a few minutes while they finished the game. "Sure, go right ahead," I said. I sat down on a sofa and looked at a magazine. After about ten minutes, the game was over, and Cynthia gave little Clyde a chocolate brownie, and parked him in front of the TV set, watching cartoons.

"He's really a good kid," she said. She didn't sound convincing. Little monster was more like it. Not a bad-looking kid. Blonde hair, a rather square face, especially around the chin; pouting lips. I had a strange feeling that the boy looked like somebody I knew. But I couldn't put my finger on *who* this could be. I mentioned this to Cynthia: "You know, the kid reminds me of somebody, his face, his features, but I can't remember who."

"He reminds you of somebody? Really? That's strange."

"Can't be Daisy or Clyde. After all, he's adopted, why should he look like them? But there's something about his face—the shape ... the chin especially—maybe it'll come to me later."

"Never mind that, Frank. Anyway, he's glued to the television set now; and he's got finger-paints in there too, and the brownie I gave him. He'll leave us alone for a while."

"I didn't appreciate the kick in the shins," I said.

"Oh Frank, I'm so sorry. He's got a lot of goodness in him. But they do spoil him," Cynthia said. "I've tried to talk to Daisy, but she's so crazy about the kid, she won't listen. He's a perfect angel, as far as she's concerned. And big Clyde isn't much better, about child-rearing. But I've got more important things to talk to you about. Do you want some coffee? Or something to drink?"

"No thanks, Cynthia. Tell me, what's on your mind?"

She sat down on an easy chair, at one side of the room, so she could watch Clyde Jr. in the next room, the room with the TV set, out of the corner of her eye. She had a worried look on her face. "I don't know if I should say anything, Frank. I have nothing concrete to go on. But I'm, well, uneasy. I have the feeling, something awful is going on. At least I think so. I have to talk to somebody, and I don't know who. And I know everything I say to you, is confidential. And you seem sensible, Frank; I think maybe you can help me."

"Cynthia: please! Get to the point."

"It's about Daisy. That's why I can't talk to anybody in the family. She's ... been acting very strange lately. Edgar's death ... it had a big impact on her."

"That's only natural, Cynthia," I said. "Somebody you know well, and he's murdered. And on top of the other thing, the other murder. Anybody would be unsettled."

"Frank, trust me: it's more than that. I mean, I'm upset, we're all upset. But Daisy, I have to tell you, she isn't a very stable person. You didn't know that. She's had, uh, certain episodes...."

"Episodes? What kind of episodes?"

"I don't just mean fits of depression. She has those too. But—once, she just plain ran away. It was, well, bizarre. She packed up and left. We didn't know where she was. We were frantic, as you might imagine. After a year, she came back. And now, she's just not herself these days. I've asked her, what's wrong? But she won't tell me. The worst of it is, I wonder if she's having an affair. I can't be sure, but I can't help wondering. We're sisters, and we're close—maybe—but there are some things she won't talk about, and this kind of thing—she locks me out completely. Totally."

"Lots of people have affairs," I said. I don't know why I said that. I suppose it's true, statistically, but most of the people I know *don't* have affairs. Or maybe they do, and I'm oblivious. Celia always tells me I have no instinct whatsoever for human relations. She might be right. Somehow she *senses* when things are wrong in a relationship, and frankly I never do. Not until it's obvious to everybody.

"Lots of people may have affairs," she said. "But they're not my sister. They don't live in the same house with me. And Clyde—well, it wouldn't be fair to him. He's a good husband, a devoted husband. And this isn't the first time, by any means. Daisy: she's not promiscuous, but she's weak, and, well, she and Clyde—I mean, he's crazy about her, but whether she's crazy about him, I just don't know. OK: I do know. She isn't."

"She doesn't love him?"

"Oh, maybe she does. But not the way he loves her; and then there's the question, if there's somebody else, who is it?"

"Her, uh, lover, is that what you mean?"

She nodded. "You know, Frank, at first I thought: maybe it's Edgar...."

"Edgar!"

"Don't sound so shocked, Frank. This is California. You didn't know Edgar well, did you? I did. I was married to the man. Let me tell you, he was rotten to the core. Marrying him was just about the dumbest thing I ever did. He had no sense of right and wrong. None whatsoever. So why did I marry him? Who knows. Why does anybody marry anybody? And Edgar had, well, something. Maybe it was sex appeal. He always had a lot of women, he attracted them like—like flypaper attracts flies. For God's sake, he attracted *me*. I fell for him like a ton of bricks. And, I felt, there was always tension over Edgar, between Daisy and me. I already told you, Daisy hasn't been a model wife. She and Clyde have had serious issues. Maybe I should say, *she* had the issues. Clyde would do anything for her. He'd kill for her, I swear."

She saw the shocked look on my face and she immediately recanted. "I didn't mean that literally.... It's just an expression, Frank."

I nodded, and told her I understood. She went on: "Anyway, as I said, she's been acting strange. I mean, even before all this. It started a while back. Don't ask me for exact dates. She seemed ... secretive, among other things. It flashed through my mind, she's cheating on Clyde. I suspected it was Edgar, but now I think maybe it was somebody else. And then—there was an incident. We were home, Daisy said she was going out to mail some letters, did I have anything I wanted to mail? She had a bunch of letters in her hand, I guess they were bills she was paying, and other stuff. I said, no, thank you. She went out the door, and when she was gone, the phone rang, and I answered it. I said hello, and a man's voice said, 'Hello, who is this? Is this Daisy Winters?' He had an accent, too. And I said, no, this isn't Mrs. Winters, this is her sister Cynthia, and can I take a message. Well, he said, how about Mr. Winters? I said, he isn't home. And he kept asking, when will either of them be home, and I just didn't like the tone, I said, I have no idea, is there a message? He said, just tell them Vladimir was on the phone, and I'll be calling them again. Then he just hung up. And when Daisy came back, I asked her, who is Vladimir?—he called and asked for you. And she said: I don't know anybody named Vladimir; but then she saw my face, and I said, well, sister dear, he certainly seemed to know you ... or Clyde, or both of you. And then she said: oh, of course, Vladimir; he's somebody that works for the hairdresser, it was about an appointment. I forgot completely, yes, his name is Vladimir, he cuts my hair.

"Of course, that was a total lie. Not a very good one, either. I mean, why would a guy from the hairdresser ask for Clyde? But, just to make sure, I called up the salon she goes to, I go there myself, and I asked for Vladimir. They said, who? I said, a foreign guy, he cuts hair. Then Fabian, he's the owner, he's the one who always does my hair, he came on and he said, Cynthia darling, we've got a Carlos and we've got a Francesco, but we don't have any Vladimirs, I'm awfully sorry; why should we have a Vladimir, but darling if you want a Vladimir, I'd be glad to hire one."

"Did you confront Daisy?"

"No, Frank, I didn't. I just thought, it's none of my business, I'll let it drop. I was worried, but I didn't see what I could do. And then I more or less forgot all about it. But when you mentioned Vladimir ... that the dead man was named Vladimir, well, what was I supposed to think? Of course, it could be a coincidence, but I don't think so. And that made me wonder—maybe he was Daisy's lover, and he wanted to talk to her, and then to Clyde too. I thought, he's going to confront Clyde, and so maybe Clyde got jealous and killed him. I hate myself for even thinking that. It was an evil thing to think. But I couldn't drive it out of my mind, that maybe Clyde knew him, and killed him, and then he got rid of all the identification—and maybe Daisy, maybe she lied too.... Am I crazy, Frank?"

I said, "No Cynthia, certainly not crazy. I mean, what you say, it could be true, I suppose. But we don't have anything to go on, really. And maybe there's some other explanation. There's more than one Vladimir in the world. You're really jumping to conclusions."

She said: "I know that. I feel so helpless. I can't bring it up, obviously, with anybody here, in this house. But it's so weird, this feeling, maybe my brother-in-law is a killer. Clyde isn't the type, I know that. He's not a bad man. He's a good man, he's decent and all that ... but Daisy is his obsession. He's wild about her, it's almost pathological."

"Wild enough to...."

"Kill? I just don't know. No, it just doesn't seem in character. Not really. But, I have to say, he would do absolutely anything not to lose her. Short of ... oh God, I don't know, Frank. This sort of thing—I mean, killing somebody—would be so ... extreme. You know, since you told me about this Vladimir, I've had these awful thoughts, things running around in my head. Not just about Clyde, but also ... heaven help me, about Daisy—"

That startled me. "Daisy? In what regard?"

"Oh God, Frank. Maybe *Daisy* killed him. To get rid of him. Maybe she was through with him, and he ... he wouldn't let go. Daisy—it would be more like her than Clyde. Oh, I hate myself for saying this. But Daisy, she's so unstable—sometimes, the way she behaves. Like the time she disappeared...."

"You mentioned that."

"It was awful. I told you, we had no idea where she was. Clyde was absolutely frantic.... She was gone for almost a year, I think. We knew she was OK, she sent Clyde a message, actually messages, I don't know what all of them said, but basically, according to him, the messages said she was OK, but we were not to look for her, or trace her, she just needed time. Oh God, do you think she went off with this Vladimir? Or somebody else? But she did come back."

"And when she came back? What did she say?"

"Nothing. She refused to talk. It was a closed book. Maybe she talked to Clyde, but I doubt it. She just ... it was, like, here I am, take it or leave it. Don't ask questions. But now, with these murders—Frank, what should I do? What can I do? Should I go to the police?"

"With what, Cynthia? This is all conjecture," I said. And of course I wanted nothing to do with the police. They might start asking questions about tan jackets. That was a ridiculous thought, I know that, but I couldn't help myself.

"You're so right, Frank. And I don't want to do anything that would hurt my sister. Or Clyde. But don't I have a duty to say something? They haven't identified the man in Lytton Park. If we told them, his name was Vladimir, and he was Russian, maybe that would help."

"Cynthia, please don't do that," I said. "Maybe they know already, who he is. I just don't want to get involved. I would have to tell them, that I heard it from Melissa Funk, or you would have to tell them you heard it from me; I just don't want that. And you would have to talk about that phone call you got, the call from Vladimir."

"I don't care about Melissa Funk."

"And I don't either, Cynthia. But, please: it would get *me* involved, and your sister and brother-in-law, and I beg of you, don't do it."

She thought about this for a minute. She was about to say something, but she had to go quickly into the other room. Clyde Jr. had gotten tired of TV, and was pulling the tail of the family cat, and the cat was screeching, and probably about to scratch the boy, which he richly deserved. She came back in a few minutes, a little out of breath and sat down. "I'll do what you say, Frank," she said. "But make me a promise. Promise me you'll try to find out what's going on here. I know, it's not your job, really. But I trust you, Frank. I heard that you're good at this sort of thing."

"I'm not. Where in the world did you hear that?"

"People talk, Frank. They say you helped crack some really tough cases."

"Cynthia, believe me, if I did, it was an accident. I'm no Sherlock Holmes. I don't do that sort of thing, and I don't want to; and I'm not good at it, really."

"You're being modest, Frank. Promise me, at least you'll try."

"OK Cynthia. I promise. But I swear, I have no idea what to do."

"Talk to people. Talk to Clyde. Not Daisy, but Clyde. Maybe he'll confide in you, and just—well, please promise, you'll think about things, you'll try to figure things out ... maybe you'll get an idea."

In her mind, I was Hercule Poirot, with his little gray cells. No doubt inside my skull there are in fact millions of little gray cells, but they can be remarkably sluggish at times. Not to mention the millions of little gray fear cells, and the shy cells, and the laziness cells. But I had to make the promise—anything to keep her away from the police; anything, frankly, to keep them from finding out I was at Edgar's house that day, that I was the furtive creature the neighbors saw from their nosy window.

* * *

But, you see, I was in a quandary. I had to do *something*; I promised Cynthia I would take some steps. What, though? When I'm in this kind of a situation, I have to bring my good wife into the picture again. So, after dinner, a nice dinner of beef stew and salad, a pleasant enough dinner even though the girls were bickering and quarreling, I told Celia I wanted to ask her advice about something.

Advice? She recognized the signs. I was in trouble. She sighed. The girls, as usual, had gone to their rooms and slammed their doors shut. They were ostensibly doing home-work, and possibly they were; but at the same time, they were sending text messages, and watching God-knows-what on their computer screens. Why did we ever buy them computers? I guess we had fantasies about educational uses of these ma-chines. I guess we pictured them learning calculus, watching King Lear, or a live performance of the Mass in B Minor. How parents can be so dumb, I cannot imagine. Of course, at this point there is no way we can undo the damage: taking the computers away would be like taking away their cell phones, which would be the equivalent of a major amputation.

Anyway, Celia and I went into the living room, and sat down together. Celia took out her knitting; and I told her the whole story—including the night at Edgar's house. I gave her all the details I had left out before.

She frowned deeply. "Frank, how can you do this? You're always keeping things from me. These things come out in dribs and drabs. I want to know, how come you never told me some of this before?"

I mumbled a lame excuse.

Once again, she talked about lack of trust, and how wrong it was to keep secrets. "Really, Frank." Once again I had to eat crow.

I needed advice, and the price—everything has a price— was, as usual, confessing my sins and exposing my poor self to her legitimate complaints.

"I was wrong, darling. I admit it. I just don't like to get you involved. You have so many things on your mind."

"That's nonsense, Frank. I know you. When you don't tell me things, it's because I won't approve. You go ahead anyway and hope I don't find out. Really, it's disgusting, Frank. How could you?"

I flagellated myself as many times as necessary, and then humbly asked her: "Now, what should I do?"

"If only you told me about this, in the first place. You know what I would have said. Do nothing. It's none of your business. Stay out of it."

"OK, but now?"

"Same advice."

"But I promised Cynthia. I can't just do nothing."

She thought about this for a second. "Well, Frank, I suppose you're right. You have to do *something*. But I really don't know what. You certainly aren't going to run around looking for a killer; and where would you look? Who do you suspect? Is it Clyde? You know him better than I do. Can you imagine him doing this? I mean, murdering two people?"

"Honestly, I can't picture it. He seems like a completely decent person."

"Well, you never know," she said. "People have been fooled before. But I think you might as well talk to him. Find out what he thinks. Ask him if he knew who this Vladimir was. I don't believe this story about Daisy and a lover for one minute. It sounds too fishy to me. There's some other explanation. And the other thing: is there some way you can find out what Edgar was involved in? He was up to no good, we know that. You should talk to his brother Roger, find out if he has anything to say."

"I don't think I'll get anywhere," I said.

"You won't," Celia said. "But at least you can tell Cynthia you tried. And then, that'll be the end of it, Frank. No more. You have a tendency to get yourself entangled in these things. I've told you time and time again, it's a bad idea."

Celia greatest virtue, and her greatest fault, was her unfailing common sense.

12

Dutifully, I put in a call to Clyde Winters, when I got to the office the next day. But he wasn't in, either at home or at work. I left messages, and told him to call me back.

The day passed normally. When I went home, and gave my report, Celia was pleased. At least I had tried. The girls were off again with friends that evening. I asked "Don't they ever stay home?" (Celia's answer was, "not if they can help it"). That left the two of us. Celia said she'd throw something together for dinner: "I'll put up some pasta, and I'll make a salad." But I said, "No, let's go out; you look tired." She didn't argue. "If it's pasta you want," I said, "we can always go to Zuppa Zuppa." That struck her as a good idea. I was thinking, of course, of the free dessert, at least if Joe was around.

He was. He was standing near the door, looking glum. He always looked glum, unless every table was full, and there was a line of people waiting to get in, plus customers sitting at the bar drinking overpriced wine or eating appetizers. And even then, he liked to complain—making people wait was bad for business, they don't come again, etc., etc.

We sat down at a table, and Joe came up to me.

"Hi Frank," he said, "good to see you."

"Business is good tonight," I said.

"I can't complain. Yesterday was dead, but tonight, it's better. Look, Frank, since you're here, can I talk to you about something? In private?"

"Well, Joe, is it important?"

"Sort of. Can you come to my office?"

It was awkward. I didn't want to leave Celia sitting by herself. But she said, "Go on, Frank, do what you have to do. Only don't take long."

We went to Joe's small, cluttered office; he waved me to a seat and said. "You know, Frank, I told you a story about me and Edgar Greenhouse. Well, it wasn't a lie, I don't like to tell lies, but I wasn't telling you the whole truth, like I should have."

I said: "That's alright, Joe. You know what you have to say, and what you don't have to say. I don't mind. Anyway, I don't want to pry into your business. Or your personal life."

"I respect that, Frank. I do. But I got to tell you something. Get it off my chest. This guy, the drunk guy, the one I threw out, it's about him. Edgar, he told me, never mention this guy again, and I said, hey, I won't. But then he comes to see me, Edgar I mean, and he said, Joe, I hate to say this, but maybe you're in trouble. I said, trouble, what kind of trouble. He said, that man, do you know who he was? I said, no, OK, so tell me.. So he says, his name is Vladimir, he's a Russian, you know that. And he could get you into trouble.

"How's that, I said. Well, he says, he's part of the Russian mafia, you know about the Russian mafia, and I said, yeah, sure, I read the papers, what do you think I am, an ignoramus? He says, you know, these guys are rich and they have connections, and they're bad guys, tough guys, really mean and vicious, you know? And he's got influence here, not just in Russia, he could go to the cops and get your license revoked. Tell you the truth, I thought he was lying, that man didn't look like Mafia to me, he looked more like a bum if he was anything, but what could I do? Edgar said, give me some money, and I can fix things up. I said, how much, he said, let's start with a couple of thousand. So I gave him money, but I knew he'd be back for more. So when you asked me, after the funeral, if Edgar owed me money, I said, the opposite. I meant I owed *him* money. And sure enough, he comes around, he says, it's not enough, we need more.... and I give it to him. But I tell you frankly, I could see, this was going to go on and on; and I prayed to God I could find some way to get rid of him, get rid of

Edgar, and somebody did take that bastard off my hands. And this Vladimir too. I mean, he was dead too. This broad, Melissa, you know, the one that Edgar was humping, she told me, Vladimir was dead. She called and told me that. I was happy. I mean, maybe he had a family, this Vladimir, everybody's got a family, Edgar had a family, they could be all broken up, you know, grief-stricken, but for me, it was like heaven."

"I can believe that," I said.

"And I wanted to tell you this, Frank, just so you know. This Edgar, he was no good. I'm glad he's dead. I went to the funeral parlor, but you know, Frank, I felt like a hypocrite. You're my lawyer. I was gonna ask you, find out if this guy really was mafia or not, could you find out, get me some peace of mind. But now I don't have to, Frank."

"I think it was all a bluff," I said. "I don't think he was mafia. Anyway, they're dead, and you can rest easy now."

"That's what I thought. So now I told you. Go enjoy your dinner, Frank. By the way, it's on the house. Not just the dessert. Ask the waiter about the specials. Whatever you want, you get. And a bottle of wine. I'm feeling generous tonight."

"Thanks, Joe," I said, and went back to the table. The special in fact was dover sole, with an asparagus risotto. To be honest, it was only so-so, but the price was right.

Celia and I enjoyed the meal. We became all mellow, somehow. A glass of red wine always helps. It was only on the way home that I stopped to think about what Joe had said. And I realized: here was somebody finally, with a genuine, honest-to-God tangible motive for killing Edgar. And Vladimir, too, for that matter. But I refused to follow out this train of thought. Joe had his problems ... but I couldn't see him as a murderer. The problem was, I couldn't see *anybody* as a murderer—at least none of the people who were involved in this case. Well, maybe Melissa Funk—she came closest. Or the mysterious Anna. But even those two didn't seem very likely.

Still, *somebody* killed those two men.

We went home and watched TV. It was one of those doctor programs: a young man comes into the emergency room, he's unconscious, his vital signs are lousy, nobody can figure out why he's dying, and there's complications, too: he has been having an affair with the wife of his next door neighbor, a weirdo who keeps exotic animals; and then the main character, doctor so-and-so, who is meanwhile having problems with the medical board because of something I can't recall, anyway, he figures out that the young guy had a rare and lethal infection, which he got from the neighbor's pet chimpanzee—which was transmitted to the neighbor's wife, but she was a carrier, who didn't get sick, only she communicated the disease to the young man during sexual intercourse.

It was a bit far-fetched, but I found it quite exciting, especially the race to get the serum that would cure the disease, which was to be found only in Atlanta at the CDC, and in the Chad Republic, but Atlanta was a better bet. The show was so engrossing that I forgot entirely about Vladimir and Edgar, except during the endless commercials, and hardly even then.

* * *

Next morning, I called the Greenhouse-Winters house again, and asked for Clyde. Daisy answered, and told me, he was out of town, on business, and wouldn't be back for a few days.

I then called Roger Greenhouse: first at his office, where a receptionist answered in very icy tones, saying Mr. Greenhouse was not available, and who was this calling, and did I have an appointment, and with which legal matter was this concerning? I decided just to hang up, which I did. I managed to get Roger's home phone number, and I called that one too. Somebody picked up, and gave me a feeble hello.

"Is this Roger Greenhouse?"

"No, this is Martin Greenhouse. Who are you?"

"I'm Frank May, the attorney," I said. "Is Roger Greenhouse available?"

"He can't speak to you now," Martin said. "He's busy."

"When will he be free?"

"Pretty soon. Can ... can you come over? If you came right now, I think you could speak to him."

I thought that was a rather peculiar way to phrase things,

but I agreed. Roger Greenhouse lived in Atherton, an extremely posh suburb just south of San Mateo, where my office is located. In Atherton, the streets are lined with beautiful old trees, the houses are discreetly set back from the streets, and absolutely no stores, businesses, or other excrescences of the workaday world are allowed to intrude. I suppose you don't absolutely have to be rich to live in Atherton, but I don't know how else you could afford to buy a house there. Maybe you might have inherited it. Or bought it years ago, before the housing bubble.

Roger had one of the smaller houses on his block, but it was nonetheless very impressive. The house had a big, beautiful garden in front, which must have cost a lot to maintain, since I assumed that Roger Greenhouse himself was unlikely to put on work-gloves, pull up weeds, spread mulch, and tend to the compost heap.

I rang the bell. Martin answered the door. He said, "Come in." I entered a large living room, impeccably furnished in a way that screamed: "A decorator was here and did me!"

Martin sat down awkwardly on a chair. I reintroduced myself, and said, "Can I speak to your brother, now?"

"He isn't here."

"But you said...."

He had a kind of stammer, and when he spoke, he mumbled, which made it even harder to figure out what he was saying. "I—I told you a lie, Mr. May. I'm sorry. But please don't be angry. I had to talk to somebody ... a lawyer. I need a lawyer, badly...."

"Where's your brother?"

"He's gone. He won't be back until Friday. Please. I have to talk to you."

"Look here," I said, "you told me—"

He never looked me in the eye. I don't think he ever looked anybody in the eye. He seemed to be staring at something on the floor, but this was just his way, I suppose. "I know I told you.... but, Mr. May.... I'm so unhappy ... I don't want to be trouble, but like I said, I have to speak to a lawyer...."

"Your brother's a lawyer."

"He won't help me. I'm really desperate. I've got to find her, Anna, the Russian lady; she's gone, and I have to find her. Can you help me?"

"Anna? How could I help you? I have absolutely no idea where she is. Anyway, why is this so important?"

He didn't answer right away. He seemed to be having trouble getting the words out. "Because... I think she's pregnant and ... I think it's my baby...."

Oh Lord. Still, I didn't see how I came in to the picture, and I told him so. He stuttered and stammered, saying he thought a lawyer could help him; he could barely get the words out, and his palms were sweaty. A lawyer could make sure he had his rights, his rights to his baby: that was the gist of what he was saying.

Again I said: "Did you talk to Roger? He's your family. Why don't you get him to help? Are you embarrassed, or what?"

"I can't do it. Roger laughs at me. He told me to forget all about it. How was I supposed to forget? And—it was all Edgar's doing, in the first place, he told me, I could have her, I could have sex with her, I'm not great with women, but—then, later on, when she went away, I told Roger all about it, and he just laughed when I talked to him, and he said, Martin, you big baby, don't tell me you actually like that broad, and I said, yes Roger, I do, I really like her. I never had much of anything before, and he said, well, just forget about her, forget the whole thing. She's gone back to Russia. But I don't believe him. I said, why should she go back to Russia, she doesn't like it there, she told me that, she said, she likes this country; and he said, well, anyway, about the baby, she's not the mother type. She'll just get an abortion, how about that, Martin? And I said, I don't want her to, isn't it my baby too. And he said, just shut up and mind your own business; she'd just make a fool of you."

He was sobbing now. You had to feel sorry for the guy. He asked me, did I think she would have an abortion?

"Martin, I don't know the woman. I suppose she could."

"I don't believe it," he said. "I think it's something else. I think she's going to have the baby, my baby, and I said so. And

Roger said, well, what of it? If she has it, then, she's just going to sell it, and I said, Roger, you can't sell babies, and he just laughed at me some more. So I'm asking you, is that true? Can you sell babies?"

"Not exactly. I mean, no, you can't sell babies. Not legally."

"Roger said you could. He said, either way, forget about her. It hurts me when he laughs at me. I'm a human being, I have feelings. Sometimes he's nice, I mean, I need Roger ... and ... he helps me out sometimes. But then—Mr. May, I think I'm kind of going crazy, I'm so upset. Roger—he must be lying.... if she came back, or if you found her, couldn't I get my rights, couldn't I try to prove, the baby is mine?"

I told him he I was no expert, but that, yes, if the baby was his, he really would have some rights. I sat him down, and as calmly as I could, I explained what I knew about the fathers' rights, in cases like this. I don't know if he understood a word of what I was saying. Probably not. And of course, a good legal case was not enough: first he had to find the woman, and she had to give birth. If she did have an abortion, he was helpless. I told him that there was nothing I could do. I had no way of finding Anna. I suggested he hire a private detective, but somehow I felt it would not happen. Maybe he was too much under his brother's thumb. Or too torpid to take action.

Strange how many people seemed to want me to do things I just can't do, won't do, and am unqualified to do.

I left the house with a feeling of deep failure. But when I thought over what Martin had said, I realized that Roger knew more about this affair, than he had ever indicated to me. When he came to see me, he gave the impression he had no idea who Anna Petrovna was—just a name he found in his brother's files. But either he had found much more out, since then; or else he was lying at the time. In any event, this Anna was at the heart of the whole bloody mess. And she was gone.

13

Nonetheless, I had a pleasant, uneventful weekend. Maybe pleasant and uneventful are related. Celia and I saw a movie, something about a single mother, who is trying to decide which of several boyfriends to choose. In the end, of course, as we know, she chooses the one she hated in the beginning—the one played by the most famous movie star. I slept through much of the movie, but still it was great to get out of the house.

I remembered that Clyde was supposed to be back in town on Tuesday. So Tuesday I followed Celia's advice, and called him again.

This time he was in. "Clyde: it's Frank, Frank May. How are you doing?"

"Tired. Jet lagged. I just came back from New York."

I said: "Look, can we get together? There are some things I want to discuss."

"Oh? Anything important?" His voice dripped with suspicion. I told him it was legal business, which was more or less true; and also some new developments, in the two murder cases; and of course that got his attention, as I knew it would. Clyde said he was free for lunch, and we met in downtown San Mateo. I talked him into my favorite Chinese restaurant, the Mandarin Dragon. I was a little apprehensive about this upcoming conversation, and I figured the least I could do to make it palatable, was to pamper myself with Chinese chicken salad and prawns in black bean sauce.

Quickly, we got down to business. I told Clyde that we now knew the name of the man in Lytton Park; his name was

Vladimir, and he was Russian. I also told him that we had reason to believe that somebody in his house, maybe him, maybe Daisy, knew something about this Vladimir. I went on: "There could be two people named Vladimir, it's not that rare of a name, in Russia anyway, and there's plenty of Russians around here. But frankly, Clyde, I don't believe it's a coincidence. So, what I was wondering, are you the one who knew this Vladimir, or was it Daisy, or what. I wanted to talk to you first, and then maybe later, I might talk to Daisy."

That seemed to upset him. "Please, Frank, leave Daisy out of this. She, well, she hasn't been well lately, and—and I don't want to burden her. But why—don't get me wrong—why are you asking these questions? I mean, you're—I mean, how does this involve *you*, Frank?"

I decided to tell the truth. "Cynthia is my client. I'm trying to help her."

"Help her? How? I don't quite get it."

Here I stumbled a bit. "You have to admit, Clyde, the situation—I mean, the dead man, and he had your address and phone number—and now Edgar, who used to be a member of your family, you know, I mean, he was Cynthia's husband. It's not a normal situation. Cynthia's terribly disturbed about this."

"Frank, we're *all* disturbed; it's only natural. But I still don't see the connection. You're Cynthia's lawyer, but ... did she ask you to do all this? I don't think she did. And anyway, why are you so involved? Where's the legal angle?"

I had to improvise. "Well, it's not exactly a legal angle. Cynthia, after all ... you have to understand, there's a certain amount of suspicion...."

"Suspicion? Of Cynthia? What sort of suspicion? Suspicion of what?"

"Well, two deaths—"

"Cynthia? That's totally crazy. Are we talking about the same person?"

"*You* think it's crazy, *I* think it's crazy. But that's because we know her. The police, they don't know her. Just think of how it all looks. First, this man in Lytton Park. Dead. Murdered. Has an address and phone number; it's Cynthia's—"

"And mine. And Daisy's. And Mose's."

"Granted. But now, there's another death. It's her ex-husband. They had, uh, quarreled, it wasn't your friendly divorce. The police, that's the first person they'd think of, the ex-wife."

"Oh, I can't believe it," he said. "They can't be that stupid. And ... I'm still wondering about your role in this, Frank. You're no detective."

"You're right, I'm not—"

"So why are you mixing in?"

I had no convincing answer. I repeated what I said, that I promised Cynthia I would help her out; but I don't think he bought that argument. I thought, I've bungled it again, I'm too amateurish, here's another abject failure. I thought Clyde would just brush me off. Even the food seemed tasteless at this point.

But, to my surprise, Clyde took another tack entirely. He said, "You know, Frank, you're not telling me the whole story. That's obvious. There's something more here, and I don't know what it is. Maybe you're even telling the truth. But I'm not going to give you a cross-examination. I know Cynthia trusts you. I want to trust you too. Can I do that?"

"Trust me? Absolutely, Clyde."

"That's good. Listen, Frank, I want to share something with you. Actually, well, family secrets. I think, well, you're an honest guy. Discreet, right? And this will be confidential—lawyers have this confidentiality thing, don't they?"

"They do. On professional matters."

"OK. Let's say this is professional. Maybe if I talked to you, openly, you'd understand the situation better. Some of this is going to have to come out, anyway. Two people are dead, and one of them was Edgar. Let me begin, Frank, by telling you something about—about my marriage. Marriages are complicated—you know that, you're a married man. I want to tell you, first off, as syrupy as this sounds, maybe even old-fashioned, but I'm really in love with my wife. I can't imagine life without her. I love her desperately. Maybe even too much—maybe it's pathological, but there it is. From the first day I met her, I fell in love. I had to have her, it was an obsession. But Daisy: she liked me OK, but she didn't love me. She really didn't want to marry me. But she was on the rebound from—let's say, from another guy. She was miserably unhappy. I was a kind of safe harbor. So I talked her into it, and we got married.

"It was great—for me. I was wildly happy. Daisy wasn't. She has trouble, in general, with happiness. I don't think she's ever been happy. A couple of years went by and—things started to turn sour. For Daisy anyway. She was more and more unhappy. It made me frantic. The main thing was, we didn't have kids. She wanted a child, more than anything else in the world, and—we couldn't have them. It made her bitter, really bitter.... So that was a kind of shadow, you know, something that was hanging over us. We consulted doctors, sure, but, well, nothing worked. She was obsessed, and the situation got worse and worse. Where were the babies?"

I nodded my head. I remembered one of our neighbors, married to an accountant: no children. They had been married ten years, two miscarriages. She used to burst into tears, just looking at a baby. It was truly pathetic. After a while, they moved away. I don't know what happened to them. Maybe they adopted a child.

He went on: "This situation, well, it was ruining our marriage. And then she left me, Frank. She packed her bags and went away. I was beside myself. I came home, one day, and she was gone. No note, nothing. But she—she must have talked to Mose. She always had a thing for him; she was capable of great love, Daisy, when she set her mind to it, and she was really fond of him. She must have spoken to him before she left. He said to me, Clyde, I know this hurts, but try to understand. She needs the space. I told him, I can't live without her. And he said: be patient. Try. I asked him, where did she go? And can I talk to her, write to her? He said, she went to Arizona, she went to be with her mother. Her mom had cancer, I knew that. She was at some clinic in Arizona. I begged him, and I begged Cynthia, let me communicate with her in some way; but they told me, no, Clyde, you can't....

"Then Cynthia said to me, her mother was dying; and she

went to Arizona, too. And their mother did die. They shipped the body back here, and they had a funeral, but Daisy never showed up. I think the whole thing was a lie, I mean, the story that Daisy was with her mother. I think she was someplace else, but I didn't know where. I was so miserable, I was losing weight, I was frantic; I almost gave up hope. She was gone maybe ten months, maybe a year. And I missed her every day. I think I would have gone crazy, but there were people who helped me, supported me: Cynthia, but mostly Mose and Claude. Claude especially. He was so great, you don't know how great it is to have a brother like that, I don't know if you have a brother, Frank; we're twins, it's like we're the same person, we're so close. Claude told me, never lose hope, he said, she'll be back. And I wondered, did he know something? He said, for sure she'll be back.

"Maybe he did know something. And she did come back. One day, she called me, on the phone, and she said, she was coming home. I said to her, you don't know how I missed you; and she said she missed me too. I said, I thought I had lost you, forever. She said, I'll be there in a day or so, Clyde, but there's one condition, and you've got to agree to it. And I said, anything, anything, whatever it is. And she said, OK, it's this: never ask about this year, where I've been, what I've done. She said to me, I don't want to talk about it, it's a closed book, it's over and done with. I've honored her request. I can't help wondering, but I never pressed her, never asked questions. And besides, when she came back, we decided to adopt a child, and I was excited, because I knew, that would be fabulous for Daisy.

"Adopting wasn't easy. It's hard to adopt babies these days, and I said, I'll do anything, let's go to China, Bolivia, Vietnam, Romania, any place, I don't care. But in the end, we didn't have to go, we got this baby right here in the good old USA. And Daisy, she's mad about the kid, it's her whole life, it means everything to her; and it's saved our marriage, it really has. I mean, don't get me wrong, I love our son, he's the joy of my life, but for Daisy, he's more than that, he's the sun and the moon and the stars, if you know what I mean.

"So you must be wondering: why I'm telling you this, why

am I giving you this whole long story. And the reason is this: because, in some strange and mixed-up way, it has something to do with Edgar."

"Edgar?"

"Edgar. He and Cynthia, they were married, you know that; and, well, about this time, they were breaking up, he was drinking heavily, and I could see, it was coming to an end, the marriage. But they were still together, more or less, when Daisy did her disappearing act, and…. once when I was begging Cynthia to let me call her, talk to her, anything, and she was saying, no we can't do that, he came into the house, the apartment they were living in, and … I can't put my finger on it, but there was something really weird going on…."

"Weird?"

"Don't ask me what—but, I had the feeling, from things he said, and the way Cynthia reacted, the way her whole body stiffened: I had the feeling he knew where Daisy was, and—I had a deep, dark suspicion, that she had gone away with him; oh, I know, that's crazy, she was supposed to be in Arizona, and he was here. But was she really in Arizona, I never knew that for sure, and I became convinced that there was something going on between the two of them, but I didn't dare ask Cynthia, even though she must have known if it was true or not. And there's something else: when we were discussing adoption, and exploring alternatives, she said we needed a lawyer, he can arrange things, and Daisy, she insisted on Edgar. You've got to use Edgar, she said, he'll handle it, and I didn't want to, I said he's a drunk, and he's incompetent, but she said, it's Edgar or nobody. He knows where to get babies. And in fact, he did locate a newborn baby, a boy, and he said, this is it, the mother has signed off, take it or leave it; and of course, we had to go along and we did. And why not? Here was this beautiful newborn boy, and the mother had signed off. It was all legal, we adopted him, and he's ours, legally ours."

I still wasn't sure where this was heading; and why he felt he needed me, or at least needed to talk to me. But then he said: "I still don't know, for sure, I mean, if there was some-thing between her and Edgar, but suppose there was, and—and it came out, you know, then I'd be a suspect, wouldn't I? I mean, I'd be the one with the motive."

"Clyde," I said, "OK: you're right. You'd have a motive, but, in the first place, are we sure that it's going to come out? Very likely it won't. And anyway, even if somebody did find out, well, just having a motive, that's not enough; lots of people could have motives. Edgar—well, he was kind of shady. He owed people money. There must be lots of people we could point to, people with motives. And, besides, where's the evidence? There has to be evidence, they just can't say, he had a motive, he must be the one."

"Well, actually," he said, lowering his eyes, "there's something more...."

"More?"

"This man—the one they're looking for, the one the neighbors saw—the man at Edgar's house—Frank: it was me."

"You?" I sounded terrifically surprised; and I *was* surprised—more than he could possibly imagine. "How could it be you, Clyde? You don't mean you were there? At Edgar's place?"

"This is confidential, Frank: I *was*. I was there."

"But Clyde, what on earth were you doing there?"

"That's something I can't tell you, Frank. Not now. Please don't ask me. But yes, I was there. I went there for a reason—never mind. There were things I had to discuss with him. I knocked on the door.... And ... nobody answered. I noticed the door was ajar. I went inside, and I looked around, and I saw him. He was lying on the floor, and I realized right away he was dead. I panicked, and just ran. I got out of there as fast as I could. I thought nobody saw me, but I guess I was wrong. The people in the house, the big house, they saw me."

I sat there, dumbfounded, listening. I wondered, how many people were at Edgar's that night? It was like Grand Central Station. Clyde, me, later on Martin, and—somebody else, too: the actual killer. Unless of course Clyde was lying.

He went on: "So far, I've been in the clear. They didn't see enough to make any sort of identification. Funny thing, though, their description, what the nosy neighbors said, it doesn't fit me, you know, the height, the color of the clothes, the tan jacket, that sort of thing. They got it all wrong. I wasn't wearing *any* jacket. I don't even own a tan jacket, and they didn't get the color of the hair right either."

I wasn't surprised of course. After all, it was *me* they saw, not Clyde. Naturally, I didn't say a word about that.

"I guess I shouldn't find it so crazy," he said, "eyewitnesses, they always get things wrong. I read that someplace. In college, they show you how that happens, in psych classes. They do this experiment, somebody walks in, quickly, and then walks out; and then they ask the class, who was that. And let's say it was a tall woman dressed in pink, half the people will say a short woman dressed in blue or something like that. That's a comfort to me, that they got the description so wrong. But I can't help worrying: suppose somebody else saw me. Or my car, it was parked nearby, suppose they wrote down the license plate number. And I've been wondering, Frank—that's why I came to you, for advice. What should I do? I can't go to the police with my story, I just can't."

"Why not?"

"That's the point. I—don't want to tell them everything I know. Just like I can't even bring myself to tell *you* everything, Frank."

"OK, Clyde," I said. "I have to say something. About that last point, like, the way you put it, you can't bring yourself to tell me everything. I can't force you, it's your decision. But I do wish you'd open up, I really do. Let me ask you one question, and I hope you'll answer it. This guy Vladimir—the dead man in Lytton Park—the Russian guy: was that somebody you knew? Or somebody Daisy knew?"

"Why do you want to know?"

"Because I don't believe in coincidences. Here's this Russian guy, he's been killed. He has your address and phone number, and he's somehow connected to Edgar; and then Edgar is killed. I mean, there has to be a connection."

"If you say so."

"Come on, Clyde. Don't be coy: did you know this man?"

"Maybe."

"Did Daisy know him?"

"Maybe. Look: I'm not ready to talk about it. That's... that's the part I just can't discuss right now, so please don't ask me."

"Clyde: I have to ask you this—was there some sort of romantic thing going on? Was it Daisy? With this guy Vladimir, rather than Edgar?"

He hesitated. "I've been pretty open with you, Frank: up to a point. I let you know there was a delicate family situation here. But I can't really go any further. Not now."

"OK, Clyde, it's your call. And of course everything you said is confidential. I gave you my advice, such as it is. And if there's trouble, with the police, or anything like that, I can at least recommend some people."

"I appreciate that, Frank."

There was a bit more desultory conversation, but I learned nothing new; and neither did Clyde. When he left, I sat there wondering: why did he come? It was not at all clear. Did he want to find out if I knew anything?

It was hard to dislike Clyde. He was earnest, serious, a little bland, but still, he seemed like a decent, honorable man. And a good family man. That's an expression you don't hear very much anymore. It was the highest praise my mother could give somebody: "he's a good family man." I think she would forgive an axe-murderer, if he didn't fool around, treated his wife with respect, and brought home a decent income.

So: Clyde: maybe he was that rarity, the murderer who was a good family man, the murderer my mother would approve of. Like the gangsters in the movies, *The Godfather*, movies like that. Or TV shows about gangsters. They go off and murder some hapless creature, for whatever reason, and on the way home they stop in the supermarket to buy tomato sauce for the wife. Maybe Clyde was like that. Did he kill Edgar? And if he did, why? And Vladimir? There was all this loose talk about Daisy and her lovers; I don't know if I believed any of it. She hardly seemed like the type. More likely to be frigid, than a woman who went hopping from bed to bed. And, with all this talk about Edgar, and now Vladimir, the notion that she had *two* lovers, besides a husband? That just seemed like sheer fantasy.

Well, fantasy at least to me. God knows what goes on these days, I mean, as far as peoples' sex lives are concerned. If you believe what you see on TV or read about in the magazines, there is a positive sex epidemic these days, especially for young people. Everybody having all sorts of sex, dozens of lovers, amazing sex marathons, one night stands, two night stands, sex clubs, upside-down and sideways positions, and who knows what else. You read about basketball players who have so much sex you wonder when they have time to shoot baskets. Maybe all this frantic activity is confined to a few younger people and a group of aging hippies, and the rest of us are just boring and ordinary. But what do I know?

Even kids seem to know everything about sex, these days. Do they *do* everything? My daughters, for instance? I try never to think about it. Too painful. And they, for their part, probably consider the two of us, me and Celia, one step removed from Trappist monks. I wonder whether they have friends whose parents are whatever they call swingers these days. To be sure, divorced parents are a dime a dozen. I don't know about parents with lovers. I asked my older daughter vaguely about something of the sort, did she have friends whose parents lived with somebody, but they weren't married, or had mothers with boyfriends, and all I got in return was a withering look of total contempt.

But I had my legal work to do, and I couldn't spend time wondering about peoples' sex lives. I drafted a trust agreement, spoke to my client who owned a tanning salon, and finally got hold of Roger Greenhouse. I asked him if it was possible for him to come see me, and we agreed on a time, the next day.

14

I had a wretched night's sleep, possibly because of an encounter with a very spicy curry, and I dragged myself somehow to work. I was day-dreaming and waiting for Roger to show up, when my reverie was interrupted by, of all people, Sandra Saunders. She burst in like a whirlwind, and began a long speech about "exploitation."

She seemed to think I was one of the exploiters. I denied it, although I was having trouble concentrating, and had no idea what she was talking about.

"Weren't you involved in hiring Vic?"

"Vic? Who is that?"

Vic, as she reminded me, was the Filipino who, with his wife Maria, was now living in Zack's apartment, and taking care of him. Doing a great job, too, from all I heard.

"The pittance you're paying him...."

"Excuse me," I said, "I'm not paying him anything. He's not my responsibility. Why don't you take it up with the family?"

"How far would I get? They're like the rest of you, they're only too happy to take advantage of these poor souls. All these people want to do is work, earn a little money, send it back to their families.... Do you know about the history of the Philippines? First we sent an army in there, took over the country, tried to destroy the culture, exploited them outrageously; and now, when they're starving and helpless, we *allow* them to change our bedpans, for something like minimum wage—"

"Sandra, you're barking up the wrong tree. I have nothing to do with it."

"Oh, you don't? What about this dead man, the Russian? You had nothing to do with him, either?"

"Good grief, you're not suggesting I killed him."

"Not literally," she said.

"I didn't kill him metaphorically either," I said. "Sandra, please, be reasonable."

"You're connected with that rotten family. You're their lawyer. You know what I think? I think Edgar Greenhouse was running some kind of smuggling ring for aliens."

"Sandra, that's ridiculous."

"I think they smuggled this man, this Russian man, into the country, and they smuggled in this woman Anna too. I think it's a conspiracy. Maybe the mafia killed him, maybe he double-crossed them, and that's why they did it. He was a human trafficker, that's what he was. Him and that brother of his, the one who lived with him."

"You mean Martin?"

"Is that his name? Martin. That's the one. Why don't the police question him? He lived in the place, he was probably in this up to his ears."

"Sandra, really, have you met this guy? He's barely able to function, and you're portraying him as some sort of master criminal. It's completely absurd."

There was no stopping her. "Well, so maybe he wasn't exactly the head of the smuggling ring; he had to know all about it, didn't he? And then there's the other brother, Roger. I've been doing my homework. He's a shrewd operator, that much I know. You're not going to tell me he's an innocent lamb."

"No... but really, I don't know anything about him," I said. "Sandra, please, I just don't see the point of all of this. You're so worked up.... Who on earth put these ideas into your head? Anyway, honestly, I'm busy—I don't have time...."

"Too busy for justice? Listen: somebody killed these people, no? And why? All of these undocumented people, I ask you, who's bringing them in? And maybe this Russian, Vladimir, maybe he threatened to go to the authorities, that's why they had him killed. And Edgar Greenhouse: I'm wondering, was there another gang? Or was it people in his own gang? I'm not going to let this go."

"You're ... going to the police...?"

"The police! What's the point of that? They're corrupt, stupid, incompetent—no, that wouldn't do anybody any good. Probably they'd put *me* in jail. No, I'm going to do it on my own. I'm going to get to the bottom of this. There are organizations, there are people who will help, civil rights organizations. There's an organization that helps out immigrants. I'll go to them.... You wait and see...."

I wished her luck. After another round or two of denunciations, she left, slamming the door on the way out.

Of course, the whole thing was preposterous. And she was preposterous. But was there a glimmer of truth in what she said? No, the Greenhouse brothers were not smuggling aliens; that much I was sure of. But was Edgar, at least, dealing and trafficking in human beings—at least in one sense? Small human beings? More and more, an idea was taking hold, inside my mind. Maybe the little gray cells were finally working.

* * *

But before I could consult the little gray cells, Roger Greenhouse came in. He seemed mightily annoyed. It turned out, he had seen Sandra Saunders coming out of my office, and that was the source of his anger and annoyance. He made it clear he had strenuous objections, to anything at all that concerned that woman.

"She's a bitch, and she's insane. She has this fantasy, about a smuggling ring, something to do with illegal aliens. I never heard anything so completely crazy. I'm going to get a restraining order, I swear. She's harassing my brother Martin. I can't tolerate that. He's—well, I think you've met him. He can't take that kind of badgering."

"Your brother Martin—Roger, I don't know if you know this, but I had a long conversation with him the other day."

"You? With Martin? What on earth about?"

"I went to see you. At your house. He told me you were home, but you weren't. It was just an excuse to get me to come, so he could talk to me."

" Martin? For God's sakes, why?"

"He wanted my help."

"What kind of help? Jesus, what a family I have. Or had."

"He wanted me to trace this woman, this Anna. He said she was pregnant, and that it was his baby, and he wanted to find her."

"His baby! The poor dope. What did he think he was doing, deflowering a virgin? I'm glad at least he knows where babies come from."

"He said Edgar egged him on. With Anna. And maybe you did too."

"Me? Absolutely not," he said. "Poor jerk. Sometimes I wonder, where did he come from. Maybe he was dropped on his head as a baby. Edgar was rotten to the core, but at least he had brains. Pickled in alcohol, to be sure, but brains. Martin though—listen, it probably isn't his baby at all."

"Is she pregnant, though?"

"She is. Or was. Maybe she got rid of it, now that Edgar's dead...."

"Why is that relevant? Was it Edgar's baby? Was he the father? Is that what you're telling me?"

He seemed annoyed. "What do you care, *whose* baby it is? It probably isn't Edgar's either, I can tell you that. If anybody was going to have his baby, it'd be that bitch, Melissa Funk. And she's not pregnant, to the best of my knowledge. Probably she's post-menopausal, anyway. No, it's not a Greenhouse baby. It would be much more accurate to say it was in a way a Winters baby."

"A Winters baby? Is that what you said? What did you mean by that?"

"I'm not going to draw you a picture. It's not *literally* a Winters baby. But in a sense—Listen, if you're so interested, why don't you ask Clyde Winters about this Russian woman, Anna? He could tell you a thing or two."

And then he added—and I think this was the point of his visit—"What's more, I'd like you to ask Clyde Winters about my late brother Edgar. You seem to be the lawyer for everybody in that family. I've been going through Edgar's files, as I told you. Somebody wanted Edgar's mouth shut. And was willing to kill him to achieve that purpose."

"You're not suggesting that Clyde Winters did this, are you?"

"I'm not suggesting anything. But my advice to you is this: watch out. You're supposed to be representing the family; and you're also supposed to be trying to find out who killed these two men...." (I protested meekly, but he paid no attention.) "But did it ever occur to you, that these two things are inconsistent? I repeat what I said: you should talk to Clyde Winters. If he's willing to talk."

And with that, he got up and left.

* * *

Anna Pavlova's baby, like so much else in this saga, was strictly speaking none of my business. But the problems of the Greenhouse-Winters household were very much my business, and more so all the time. Sandra Saunders, it turns out, had hired a lawyer—her view was that lawyers were parasites, blood-suckers, bottom-feeders, but at times you have no choice but to avail yourself of a handy parasite, blood-sucker and bottom-feeder; there's no avoiding it. She filed suit against Zack, Mose, Cynthia, and Clyde and Claude Winters.

I didn't know the lawyer who was representing her. He was not somebody whose name I recognized; in my view, no reputable lawyer would take up the case. But there are lawyers who will take on almost anything. I looked him up—Melvin Reed was his name: he was a solo practitioner in Cupertino, another one of the many, many suburbs of San Francisco.

The complaint was really amazing. The plaintiff, Sandra Saunders, accused the defendants of violating every known law on the books, with the possible exception of the Federal Wool Labeling Act or the act to protect marine mammals. At least it seemed that way. It was written in a thick and impenetrable jargon. In essence, I think, it accused the defendants of offenses against various immigration laws, and the exploitation of undocumented aliens, in violation of federal immigration and labor laws, and so on. The only immediate result was that the lawsuit frightened Clyde and Claude. Reluctantly, they gave Vic, the Filipino helper, his walking papers. He had no proof that he was legally in this country. Most likely he was not. Clyde and Claude also stopped using the agency that provided them with Vic. Its personnel practices were somewhat dubious.

They engaged a different agency. Through it, they hired a more expensive caregiver, who had impeccable possession of a green card. She was a woman from Tonga who weighed what I would guess was about 400 pounds. She seemed adequate to the job, although Zack at first took a distinct dislike to her, first, on the grounds that she was way too fat, and second, because he didn't want a colored person. Fortunately, he kept these opinions mostly within the family circle. And she seemed to do the work as well as anyone had the right to expect. She was certainly reliable.

My task was to file an answer, and get the lawsuit thrown out of court, which I accomplished rather quickly. The judge thought the lawsuit was "frivolous." In the legal sense, this means it was silly and pointless, which of course it was—and that it had no chance of succeeding. I hope Melvin took the case on a contingency basis, so that lost money on the deal. On the other hand, if he hadn't, it might mean that Sandra was deeply in debt to this particular parasite, blood-sucker, and bottom-feeder—a thought I found almost equally attractive.

Alas, the troubles of the Winters family were not over. No sooner had the danger from Sandra Saunders abated some-what, than a new danger arose, this time from Melissa Funk. But I was, for a while, blissfully unaware of this fact.

Meanwhile, I solved the case. Or thought I did.

15

It came to me in a blinding flash of light. I felt like one of those people in the comic strips, when they get an idea, and a light bulb flashes over their heads.

In a nutshell, I put two and two together. Not by sitting down and thinking and thinking but, as I said, in a flash of light. The brain is a strange and wonderful thing. One idea leads to another; one memory sparks another, one nerve ending connects to another nerve ending. It all had to do with the custody case I was working on. This affair, as I told you, was a mess, legally speaking. And I had spent hour after hour doing research on the rules and the case law about custody, in the state of California. More hours, frankly, than I dared bill the client for. I represented a father, who was trying to get custody of his young daughter; this came out of one of those messy divorces, where husband and wife, or ex-husband and ex-wife, thoroughly hated each other. I find these cases really sad. And mysterious. Here were two people who once upon a time were madly in love, who kissed and hugged and squeezed and had passionate sex in and out of bed, who swore everlasting devotion. Now, nothing remains of the love, and all they have for each other is blind, insensate hatred. Resentment. Bitterness. How did all this happen?

Joshua—that was the father's name—told me that Helen, his ex-wife, was unfit to be a mother. "She drinks, she sleeps around, she leaves the kid alone in the house, I swear, a five-year-old, it's crazy. She goes to bars at night, picks up men and brings them home." I asked him, cautiously, whether he could

prove these allegations, which of course he couldn't. I wondered (to myself) how much of it, if any, was actually true. And
I wondered if his wife, Helen, was as big a problem for her
lawyer, as Joshua was to me—as difficult and as irrational.

Very likely she was. For one thing, Helen could match him
in venom. Her first line of defense was to accuse him of child
abuse, claiming that little Tiffany came back from visitations
with bruises on her thighs. These bruises, however, were
invisible to the naked eye. Her second line of defense was that
he wasn't the actual father; she demanded DNA testing, and he
flat out refused. "Legally, it's my child, Frank," he said. "It has
to be. You know, Tiffany looks just like me. Everybody says so.
They say: Joshua, she's the spitting image of you. My mother
says that all the time. Take a look at her chin. I mean, isn't that
my chin? Anyway, suppose I'm not the father, just suppose. I
say, so what. I love that little girl. What if she was adopted,
which she isn't. I'd love her all the same, even though she was
somebody else's kid, in the biology department. You follow me?
So I'm not going to allow this testing. Can they force me to do
it?" I said I thought they couldn't but that I'd have to do some
research. I didn't tell him about another possibility: that they
would somehow get his DNA, who knows how, a fingernail or a
bit of hair or something, and test it anyway.

It was in middle of worrying about Joshua and his daughter Tiffany, that I had the blinding flash of light. A number of
things came together in my mind. Poor Martin Greenhouse,
and his sex life, for one thing. His fantastic story about Anna
and the baby. A couple of famous custody cases, which I reread;
they were important food for thought. And then there was
Clyde Jr. I remembered that he reminded me of somebody, but
I couldn't place it, at the time. Now it came to me, as an
important part of that blinding flash of light. I had only seen
her once, but she was pretty unforgettable. And the kid really
looked like Anna. He really did. The more I thought about this,
the more I was sure of it. Little Clyde was Anna's baby. And
therefore....

Well, that was the problem. All of my reasoning led me
toward a conclusion which I just did not want to accept. It was

this: that Clyde Winters was guilty of murder. He had killed two people in cold blood. He killed to protect his right to his adopted son. She, Anna, was the mother, and maybe she was trying to get the baby back. Something about the adoption was fishy or defective, and she wanted the child. Or money. Maybe the problem was endless blackmail, from here to eternity. And Edgar was her partner in crime. They were robbing Zack and they were blackmailing Clyde. And Vladimir: how was he involved in this sordid affair? Was he the baby's father?

Maybe. But in any event, Clyde had the motive, and the opportunity, and nobody else filled the bill. Well, Daisy perhaps. But this was, I thought, impossible. I could not imagine Daisy as a killer. She was too much of a wreck, psychologically. That left Clyde. Everything pointed to him. But what was I to do with this theory? No, it wasn't theory, I said to myself. It was reality. It was cold, hard fact.

One answer was: do nothing. But I felt really conflicted. It was dinner-time at home; the girls gobbled their food down quickly, that is, the part of it they ate, the part where they didn't say "yuck" and push the plate away, and then they fled to their rooms as usual, to those sanctuaries where evil parents couldn't reach them. Celia and I cleared the dishes, and she was telling me something about her day at work. To be honest, I wasn't listening to her at all. She said, "Frank, you haven't heard a word I've been saying."

It was true. She said, "I had an awful day at the school. The kids were impossible, and the principal was breathing down my neck about some stupid report I never filed. But what's the point, Frank, in talking, when you just shut me out?"

I apologized and did a fair amount of groveling. I wasn't in the mood for an argument, especially when she was right and I was wrong. In any event, my depressed look had an effect on her. When Celia sees that something is *really* bothering me, she loses her capacity for anger. That happened now. She said: "Out with it, Frank. What's on your mind? You have to tell me all about it."

And I did. I had already filled her in on all the details, at our last after-dinner session. Now I told her my theory, and how and why I had come to the conclusion I had reached. She listened carefully. At the end, I could have predicted her advice. It was the usual advice: do nothing. Stay calm. Take no rash steps. I had no real proof. Yes, she could certainly see the point; she felt I must be right, everything pointed to Clyde. But still, it was something for the police to take care of, not me.

It was great advice. Such great advice that I even decided to take it. But destiny had other plans for me. No sooner had I gotten to the office the next day, when Cynthia called, and said she had to see me, things were falling apart, and she needed "wise counsel," as she put it. I said, of course, and told her to come right over. She said she would.

"What's up, Cynthia?" I asked, when she came in, all out of breath. I could see she was extremely agitated.

"I'm late for work, Frank, but I had to talk. It's been such a nightmare, ever since they found that man dead—Vladimir or whoever he was—and it only gets worse." She started to cry. I hate it when clients cry. I sat there, too embarrassed to say anything. I keep a box of tissues on my desk, mostly for reasons of allergies, rather than for crying clients, but now I reached over, got a tissue and handed it to her. She was sobbing and rubbing her hands together.

"Cynthia dear, I know it's hard on you, but is there something new, some sort of crisis?"

"Oh, it's everything.... I just can't take it. And Daisy, you know, in the best of times, she's always on the edge, but now—and the worst of all, it's Clyde."

"Clyde?"

"The police—they've been questioning him over and over.... Oh, this is crazy, Frank, but they think he killed those people. Why would he do such a thing, Frank? You know Clyde. He isn't a killer. I mean, it's absurd; and poor Daisy, she's not a strong person, you know that, she could break down completely.... I'm so frightened, Frank, I don't know what to do."

I had no idea what to say. I mumbled some platitude.

"I've got no one to talk to, Frank," she said. "Obviously, I can't talk to Clyde, or Daisy. And Mose—well, you know Mose. I just can't. I'm at my wits end, Frank. Tell me what to do."

"Do you know *why* the police are questioning Clyde?" I asked. "Do they have some, uh, evidence?"

"He won't tell me. But I think so. Fingerprints or something. Is there some way you can find out? Can you help us, Frank?"

"I'd like to, Cynthia, but what can I do?"

"Talk to Clyde, will you? Can't you represent him? He needs a lawyer. He hasn't got one, I know that; well, except for you. He needs somebody to go with him, when the police—when they question him, I think he shouldn't tell them anything. I mean, I don't know what he's been saying to them. You can't imagine what it's like in the house, the atmosphere.... Help us, Frank."

I explained to her, patiently and very sympathetically, for the umpteenth time, that I was not a criminal lawyer. This was a very specialized branch of practice, and I could recommend an excellent practitioner, somebody I trusted; but really, I was not what Clyde should be looking for. She nodded, and she seemed to understand, but she insisted that I talk to him anyway. "I don't mean about the law, or how to deal with police, and that sort of thing, Frank. I mean, talk to him, find out what this is all about. I can't live with this pressure, Frank."

"But does he want to talk to me?" I asked.

"Oh, he does. He told me he would. He knows I'm coming here to see you. I made him promise he would tell you what you need to know, and I told him you'd give him good advice, so please, Frank, promise you'll talk to him."

I promised.

"God bless you, Frank," she said, wiping her eyes. "I knew you'd come through for us."

* * *

But would I? I felt, in fact, relatively helpless. I called Clyde on the phone, at his office, and he answered. He said he couldn't talk at that point; he'd call me during his lunch hour, cell phone to cell phone.

"Cynthia wants me to speak to you, Clyde," I said.

"I know. I know."

"But Clyde, this time, you have to tell me everything. Don't hold back."

"You're right," he said, in a glum voice.

"So will you?"

He hesitated a second. Then he said: "Yes. Well, almost everything."

"Almost everything isn't good enough, Clyde."

"You're right.... When can we get together?"

"As soon as you want. But you're at work."

"I'll leave here now," he said. And in half an hour, he was at my door.

Seated in a chair opposite me, looking quite nervous and upset, Clyde wasted no time in beginning. "It's a new situation, Frank," he said, "Things have gotten, well, pretty dicey, as I think you know."

"I gathered as much, from Cynthia."

"Cynthia doesn't know the half of it, Frank. Yes, the police are pretty suspicious. They found my fingerprints, at Edgar's place. Of course, that doesn't mean anything, necessarily; I told them, yes, I'd been there, but I didn't say it was the night he died. And they don't know that fact yet, but I'm afraid they're closing in on me. They already think it's me, because of what those stupid neighbors said, even though the description doesn't fit. And then there's something else."

"Something else?"

He fidgeted in his chair. "Well, there's Melissa."

"Melissa Funk?"

"Yes—it's a kind of blackmail. No, not a *kind* of blackmail: it's blackmail plain and simple. She wants money. She says she's out of a job, she's pregnant, it's Edgar's baby, at least that's what she says; I don't even think she's pregnant—for God's sake, she must be 45 or more, if she's a day. But she says she is, and now she has no place to go, she's estranged from her family, blah blah, and she needs the money. I gave her $5,000. She said, it's not enough. I don't know if she's telling the truth about any of this, but I have no way of knowing. Cynthia doesn't know about this; neither does Daisy. I'm ... frantic,

Frank. What should I do?"

I thought a while. "Stop paying," I said. "Tell her, go ahead and report what you know. If you didn't kill Edgar—"

"I swear I didn't."

"Well, then what's the problem?"

He said: "Frank, don't be naive. I don't believe that old line, just tell the truth, and it'll be OK. Does that really work? The police, they have their own ideas, and if they make up their minds, if they think I'm the guy, they can frame me, or even if they don't, they can make my life miserable. I read about these cases all the time, in the papers; people sit in jail for years and then they get out, they were innocent, but the DA or somebody else from the prosecution kept stuff secret, like evidence that the guy didn't do it, or that sort of thing. No, I don't want to get the police involved, or the DA or whoever."

I listened and was thinking. He had sworn he was innocent. But don't they all swear they're innocent? Maybe the reason he didn't want to tell his story to the police, was that he *wasn't* so innocent. Of course, I couldn't say this out loud.

There was an awkward silence. Then Clyde said: "Frank, there's something else...."

"Something else?"

"I've been, well, lying about something. About Vladimir. I knew who he was. Daisy didn't know, at first. Until I told her. But I had to lie, I had to go through that whole charade, you know, at the morgue, I had to say, I didn't recognize him."

I wondered how many people had been lying to me. "And... did Cynthia know too? She swore she didn't recognize the man."

"She was telling the truth. She didn't know. She never saw the man before. She had no idea. But I did."

"OK," I said, "suppose you knew him; still, weren't you shocked? To see him, dead, in the morgue? You must be a wonderful actor. And why did you lie? What was the harm in admitting, you knew him?"

"In the morgue—oh, that was easy. You look at a corpse, nobody knows how you're supposed to react. But Frank, you see, it's more than that. Yes, I knew him, I knew he was around;

I had talked to him, yes. It's also that … I knew he was dead."

"You *knew?*"

"Let me explain, Frank. It's also about Edgar; Edgar called me on the phone. He wanted money, money, money. Also, he wanted to talk about the whole situation."

"The whole situation? What was that?"

Clyde ignored this. "He wanted a lot more money than I could afford. The money was for Vladimir, he said. If I paid up, he said, Vladimir would go away and not come back; and that's something I wanted desperately to happen. Don't ask me why, Frank, I'd rather not say at the moment. Anyway, Edgar said Vladimir would get in touch with me. Sure enough I got a message, come meet him in the park—Lytton Park—at night. He said, it would be quiet there, we could talk. But when I got there, I didn't see him. He was supposed to be sitting on a bench. I looked around and—and I found him, behind a bush. Dead. Honest to God, Frank, I'm not lying. He was dead when I got there. But then I did something foolish. I was panic-stricken. I didn't want anybody to know who he was. I thought, Edgar won't say anything, his mouth will be shut, and maybe nobody knows this guy, he's from Russia. I wasn't thinking straight…. I stripped the body of identification, I took every-thing, his wallet, his passport, keys, everything in his pockets, and I threw all that stuff in the Bay the next day…."

"But why did you do that, Clyde? Why was this so damn important to you? Why didn't you want people to know who he was? "

"I realize, it was crazy. I wasn't thinking. I thought, who knows him around here, anyway? Edgar, but who else? Oh, I must have been out of my mind. They would have found out, sooner or later, who he was. Obviously, I didn't know about the note he had sewn inside his pocket, the one with my address. But you know about that."

"But who was he, Clyde? And what kind of hold did he have on you?"

"Well, you know that already, Frank, who he was. He was a Russian guy. His name was Vladimir. Vladimir Petrov, I think. And … your other question: I'm just not going to answer it,

Frank. Please don't even ask me."

"He was blackmailing you, Clyde. About something. I'm your lawyer, Clyde. I think you ought to tell me."

He said nothing. I didn't really expect an answer. I think I *knew* the answer. But I had to be sure. I went on: "And Edgar? What was his role in all of this? He seemed to be all over the place; he and Vladimir, they were in it together, weren't they? You dealt with Edgar, right? He was acting for Vladimir, right?"

"Please, Frank. I asked you...."

"And this woman, Anna? What about her?"

"She was his wife, I think. Vladimir's. I mean, they were a couple, that much I know. Whether they were actually married, I'm not sure."

"And Melissa? Melissa Funk?"

"She—she was with Edgar. And she must have known the whole story."

"The whole story? Clyde: the story of what?"

He was struggling with himself, resisting me; he didn't want to open up. But I think I knew the story already. Of course, I wanted corroboration, proof that my suspicions were correct. I wasn't getting that—not directly. But his very silence meant something to me. It meant that I was right about what "the whole story" consisted of.

"Frank," he said, "I'm desperate. It's getting to me. And Daisy. She can't take much more of this. I've told you a lot. I swear I didn't kill these people. I'm willing to take a lie detector test, anything, truth serum, God knows what. But it doesn't look good for me, I know that. You mustn't tell the police about me."

"And Melissa? If she knows the whole story, as you put it, won't she be inclined to talk? You can't keep paying her, can you?"

"No, I don't have that kind of money. I'm at my wit's end, Frank. Can you help me?"

Could I? He was very persuasive, swearing up and down that he was innocent. But how could I believe him? His story was so improbable. He arranges to meet a man; he goes there, and the man ends up dead. He goes to Edgar's house. Same thing. Once could be bad luck, or a coincidence. But twice? How could I help him, if I thought—as I did—that he must be the one who killed Vladimir, and killed Edgar. Both for the same, very powerful reason. I was absolutely certain now, what the motive was, behind these killings.

And yet: I had to ask him, one more question: "Clyde: your meeting with Vladimir. Who knew about it? Who else could have been aware, that he was seeing you, in Lytton Park? I'm asking, who knew?"

"Nobody."

"You didn't tell anybody?"

"Well, maybe I told Daisy."

I didn't ask him why. "Did she tell anybody?"

"I don't think so. I asked her not to. But maybe she did, I don't know. Who would she tell? Cynthia? I doubt it. Mose? I don't see the point."

"Could she have heard it from ...Vladimir himself?"

"She never met him. I swear it. She knew who he was. But she never laid eyes on the man. I wouldn't allow it."

"You wouldn't *allow* it? Clyde, you're talking in puzzles."

He frowned. "Frank, I'm afraid it has to be this way.... I mean, puzzles. I hope someday I can tell you more. For now, you have to trust me. And I'm here to ask you an enormous favor."

"A favor?"

"It's about ... Melissa. I told her, she could get in touch with you. I told her you were my attorney, and that we wanted to get everything, well, in legal form."

"Everything in legal form? What on earth are you talking about?"

"I said, you'd draw up a contract, you'd arrange a schedule of regular payments, something reasonable, something I could afford, and we'd have it all down in black and white. That's what I told her."

I was dumbfounded. "Clyde, how could you do that? And without asking me? I absolutely can't agree to anything of the sort. You're talking about a crime. You're talking about black-mail, and this whole notion, a written contract; a blackmail contract. No, it's out of the question. I can't believe you did this."

He paused, and then said, in a dejected voice. "OK. I understand. I was just hoping—"

"For what? Clyde, this is just not something I could possibly do. For you, or for anybody. Risk my whole career? No, thank you. And besides, it's just wrong. And it wouldn't work; these things never do."

He was quiet. He seemed abashed. Then he said: "I'm sorry. I shouldn't have asked. It's only because I feel ... desperate, trapped. If you won't do it, I don't know what happens next. I really don't."

"Clyde," I said, "I think I know why you feel trapped. You're not giving me the whole story, that's clear. I'm pretty sure, though, that I do understand why it's so important to you. It's all about Clyde, Jr., isn't it? You're afraid of losing him, right? You don't have to answer that. I'm just saying what I feel must be true. I'm sorry for you, and your family. But what you ask, it's something shady, and I just can't do it. Can't and won't."

"Would you talk to Melissa? I mean, not about the contract, but just talk to her anyway?"

"No, I won't talk to her, Clyde. I'm sorry. You'll have to tell her, the whole thing is off, this business of a contract. And Clyde, maybe there's another way. Maybe you can pay her a lump sum. I don't know if that would work. Maybe your father can help; he's got some money. But, frankly, you're going to have to count me out."

He was silent again. And sheepish. But finally he said: "You're right. It was stupid to ask you. I should have known, you can't do this kind of thing. Forget it, Frank. I'll deal with it my way. I'm sorry, Frank, that I troubled you."

He got up, as if he was ready to go. His shoulders were hunched over, and he looked like a man in pain. I had a sudden thought: "Clyde," I called out. "This woman, Anna...."

He turned around. I said: "You don't happen to know where she went, do you?"

"Why should I?" he said, a bit sharply. "No, I have no idea. Why are you asking?"

"No particular reason," I said. He looked at me, as if he was about to form a question, which he then failed to ask.

He went out the door. I watched him go, and then I sat in my chair, thinking and thinking. Exactly what had I expected Clyde to say about Anna? That he was the father of the child she was carrying? Or something else? And what did Roger mean when he said, it was a Winters baby? If not Clyde, then who? Claude? But that seemed unlikely in the extreme. Did he mean something else altogether?

I was confused, puzzled. I was still convinced that Clyde had killed Vladimir and Edgar. But when I talked to him, face to face, it was hard to think of him as a cold-blooded killer. Or even as a hot-blooded killer. Still, when I remembered what his motive was, and how powerful a motive that could be—a mother or a father will kill to protect the life of a child. And they might kill, too, to prevent someone from snatching that child away.

Then I had a sudden and disturbing thought. It sent chills up and down my spine. Suppose Clyde *had* killed two men. Would he hesitate to kill again—for the same powerful reason? Besides Vladimir and Edgar, there was a third threat to their family—Melissa Funk. She was blackmailing him. She knew the whole story. He had come to me, with a plan for dealing with her, and I had refused to help him. It wasn't my problem I said. And of course it wasn't; that part was true enough. But then what was his response: "I'll deal with it my way." What way was that? Could he be planning to *kill* Melissa Funk?

If so—and even if this was only a possibility—then, despite what I told Clyde, I had a duty to talk to Melissa. I had a duty to warn her to watch her step. Otherwise, if something happened to her, it would be in a way my fault. I couldn't have that on my conscience.

I decided to act right away. I called Melissa's flat; luckily, I had written down the number. There was no answer. I left a message, asking her to call me, on my cell phone. I told her it was urgent.

But she didn't call back. Hours went by. I felt more and more nervous. I called her at ten o'clock that night. Nobody home. At midnight, when I was reasonably sure Celia was fast asleep, I tiptoed out of bed, into the living room, and made another call to Melissa's home number. Nobody answered. Just an answering machine: Please leave a message.

My tiptoeing isn't what it used to be: I made something of a clatter, when I bumped into a dresser on my way out. Celia appeared in the living room, rubbing her eyes. She was in her nightgown. She said: "Who on earth are you calling at this hour?"

"Oh, a client."

"A client? At midnight? What kind of a client is that?"

I had no answer. She said: "Frank, it's this business we've talked about before; there must be something new going on. You're a bundle of nerves, I can see that. You never tell me the whole story. You bring me up to date, but then something else happens, and I have to get it out of you with a pliers. I'll never get back to sleep, unless you tell me everything. Is there something new?"

"Well, there is, sort of," I said.

It's never any use trying to fool Celia. She knows me too well. She can read me like a book. I sat her down, in the living room, and I filled her in about my conversation with Clyde. She said: "Frank, you've got to go to the police."

"Celia, how can I?"

"Easy. Just do it. First thing in the morning. That woman, she might already be dead, Frank. Think of that."

I could hardly think of anything else. And yet.... I said, "Celia dear, it's not so easy. In the first place, if I told them about my talk with Clyde, well, it would be a breach of ethics."

"Are you out of your mind? You're talking about ethics? And meanwhile, this woman could be killed? What kind of ethics is that?"

"But Celia, I haven't got any proof."

"That's not your problem. The police, they'll find the proof. And they can send somebody over, somebody to protect this Melissa."

"If they believe me."

"Well, they can't believe you if you don't say anything. And there's another thing, Frank. You think you know why Clyde Winters killed these people. Did you ever stop to think, that he *knows* you know?"

"I don't think so. Well, maybe he does...."

"Maybe?"

I remember that I had said, foolishly, that I knew what his motive was—that it was all about little Clyde. Sheepishly I said, "I guess, uh, I guess he does know, honey. He knows I have the general idea.... But I'm not sure he knows whether I've got all the details."

"The details! Really, Frank, sometimes I wonder about you. He doesn't need to know whether you've got the details. You told him you know it's all about little Clyde; and that's the main thing, the important thing. Don't you realize what that means?"

"Not really."

She looked at me, and gave me a glance that was part anger, part fear, part contempt. "It means, Frank, that Melissa's not the only one in danger. There's also you. *You're* someone else who knows too much."

I sat there silent. Petrified.

Then I said: "Maybe if I talked to Clyde...."

"Are you stark raving mad, Frank? A murderer? You want to be his next victim? First thing in the morning, you go to the police."

"I don't think—"

"But I *do* think, Frank. Just do what I say."

I had to agree.

"Now come to bed," she said. "Don't stay up all night. You need your sleep."

But that was easier said than done. Celia fell asleep quickly. I crawled into bed beside her, but falling asleep was out of the question. Not with all those things on my mind. It was hours before I lapsed into a fitful and uncomfortable sleep.

16

What Celia said was undoubtedly true, and it disturbed me no end. How could it not? I tossed and turned for hours. Every time I tried to close my eyes, I had visions of Clyde Winters or some hit man he hired stalking me and cutting me down in my prime. They would be waiting for me outside my office, in a car with tinted glass. Or they would burst into my office with machine guns. Also, I had visions of Melissa Funk in a pool of blood, a corpse with big staring eyes, like Edgar's. I was all conscience-stricken, too, sick to my stomach, since so much of all this was really my fault.

I finally fell asleep at what must have been 3:00 a.m., and it wasn't much of a sleep, as I said. It was punctuated with nightmares and outbreaks of sweating. I think I disturbed Celia too. And when the alarm rang, at 7:00, I could hardly drag myself out of bed.

I dreaded the call to the police. But I knew I had to do something. I said to Celia, over the breakfast table: "Maybe I should go to the police station. I don't think they pay much attention to phone calls."

She said: "Just do it, Frank. One way or the other."

I reminded her I had an appointment, with a client I couldn't afford to stand up; I promised to do the bloody deed before noon. I drove to the office, driving very slowly and carefully, and watching out the back to see if some sinister black sedan was following me. No sedan appeared, and I got to the office unharmed, which I considered something of an achievement, all things considered.

It took all of my will power to get through the morning's business. My appointment was with my wealthiest client, an elderly and very eccentric lady, Mrs. Wheelwright, who had come to talk about changing her will. She did this on a regular basis. Against my advice, she, like some other clients, put in her will an elaborate scheme for distributing a whole list of gew-gaws. She spent more mental energy on this aspect of her estate, than on the problem of disposing of her stocks, bonds, and real estate—which were worth many millions. The stocks and bonds and real estate were going to various nieces and nephews (she had no children), but there was page after page of specific legacies. Here's a sample: "One strand of my pearl necklace to Minerva Hatchet, the other strand to Sylvia Backstein." And here's another: "The Meissen figurine of a shepherdess and her flock, to Emma Percival." Year by year, these provisions (as I had warned her) tended to become obsolete. She was, for example, no longer speaking to Emma Percival. The Meissen figurine, in any event, no longer existed; a careless housemaid had dropped it while dusting in the room where it stood, and it shattered into a thousand pieces. The housemaid was fired, and of course she asked me to delete the clause about the figurine (along with the small legacy to the housemaid). Then she combined the two strands of the pearl necklace into one single, very long strand, for reasons Mrs. Wheelwright never made explicit, but which might have had to do with the large and growing size of her bosom. "Now, Frank, I don't know what to do," she said. "Shall I give it to Minerva or to Sylvia? They can't both have it, you know."

I had to cope with all of this and more, while my mind, to be honest, was a million miles away. But somehow I managed.

I finally wound up my business with Mrs. Wheelwright, and she left my office. I realized that I had to make my move, which I dreaded beyond anything else.

But at this point, fate suddenly intervened. This is the sort of thing fate does: it intervenes. I was trying to pull myself together and get up the courage to go down to the police station, when fate called me on the telephone, and then, half an hour later, walked through the door.

Or rather, Clyde phoned me, not fate. He said he wanted to see me. I was reluctant. I don't like meetings with murderers. I had visions of a rendezvous with Clyde in a dark alley, or in Lytton Park, at night. Of course, if he asked for such a meeting, I would simply refuse to go. But he wanted something much more mundane; he wanted to come over to my office, and as soon as possible. I might have said I was busy, but I didn't. He said he could be there very soon.

Clyde was prompt. He came in, sat down, and began to talk. First, he said, he wanted to apologize again, for asking me to do something which, he should have known, I wouldn't and couldn't do. Then he said, "anyway, the crisis is over."

"The crisis? What do you mean?"

"I mean Melissa. She's leaving town. Maybe she's left already. The whole money thing is off. She told me so herself. I don't have to worry about it. That's what she said. She's moving, she's going far away, and that's that."

I should have felt relieved, but instead, I felt a cold chill. "What made her change her mind?"

"I don't know. Don't care, either. She just did."

"Clyde, was it money? Did you pay her anything?"

"Not a penny."

"Did Mose pay her? Did anybody pay her?"

"Nobody. I told you that. No money. Maybe she won the lottery, Frank. As I said, I don't care. She's not my problem anymore. Look: maybe she had a guilty conscience. I'm not looking a gift horse in the mouth."

I was hardly on intimate terms with Melissa Funk, but a guilty conscience didn't strike me as part of her character. Was the real motivation fear? Two people had died, because they knew the secret; and it would be no wonder if Melissa felt, she might be the third. Maybe Clyde had a conversation with her, made threatening noises, and she was frightened enough to throw some underwear into a tote-bag, and take the next plane, train, or bus out of town.

Or maybe she was dead? Murdered and dumped in the Bay?

God, I hoped not.

The crazy thing is, that somehow, for myself, I felt less afraid. Maybe this was totally irrational, but sitting here in front of me, Clyde, as always, just did not seem like a killer. And he certainly did not look like a man who was confronting his next intended victim. A person he intended to kill or frighten out of town. Of course, he could have pulled out a gun then and there and gotten rid of me, but that would be awkward, to say the least. A whole floor of orthodontists and patent lawyers would hear the noise, and see him, as he ran helter-skelter away from the scene of the crime. I said to Clyde, "excuse me a minute," and I picked up the phone and called the receptionist. She sat in the outer office of the suite, in which I rented space, along with three other lawyers. I said to her in a loud voice, "please hold my calls, I'm in conference with Clyde Winters."

She must have wondered why on earth I was mentioning the name, and why so loud, and why I was acting so peculiar. I thought of it as a kind of health insurance. But Clyde was no fool. He guessed exactly what I was doing, and he smiled—a sort of twisted smile, like the one I used to see on Vice President Cheney's face, in the newspapers. He said: "You still think I'm involved, don't you, Frank?"

"Involved? In what?"

"Oh, come on. Involved in this whole dirty business. Vladimir. Edgar. It's because you're sure you know why these men were killed.... Am I right?"

I hemmed and hawed. He said: "You think it's all about Clyde Junior, don't you?"

I don't know what possessed me, but I spoke out candidly. "I do. You want to know what I think, Clyde? I think it *is* about the baby. I think the issue here is adoption and custody. I think this woman, Anna, was the baby's mother. The kid looks like her—I realized this the other day. Am I right, Clyde?"

"I'm not going to say."

"I know I'm right. And the father? That was Vladimir, right?"

"OK. I'll admit it. This is all confidential, anyway, so what the hell. Yes, Anna was the kid's mother, and Vladimir was the father. I think they were a married couple. Or maybe not. Who gets married these days? They were living together, that's for sure. Then I think they split up, who knows why, and he went back to Russia. I think he didn't know she was pregnant. She had the baby, and she gave it up for adoption. Edgar handled the whole business. Then somehow Vladimir got wind of things, and he came roaring back to this country."

"To assert his parental rights."

"Exactly."

"And," I said, "he could maybe undo the whole adoption business. He's the father, and he never relinquished those rights. This woman, Anna, she lied to everybody. When she gave the baby up for adoption, she never said anything about Vladimir. Maybe she said, the father was unknown, or something like that. And Edgar, he lied too. But that's not the issue. Vladimir had what he thought was an iron-clad claim to get back his kid. Well, maybe not iron-clad, but he surely had a strong case. And when he got here, he used that threat to extort money out of you. And maybe Daisy, but I'm not sure of that. So there's a powerful motive for murder, Clyde. A powerful motive for getting rid of Vladimir. And getting rid of Edgar, too, for that matter. Edgar knew the adoption process was flawed, and he was desperate for money. Maybe he was doing a bit of blackmail himself. So that's what I'm thinking, Clyde. That's my theory."

"You're accusing me of murder."

"Not exactly, but—"

"What does 'not exactly' mean? I either did or I didn't kill those people. Admit it. You think it's me."

I refused to answer.

He said, "Anyway, Frank, you think the police don't know this story?"

"I don't know," I said. "Maybe they do, maybe they don't. But am I right? Did I get the story right?"

"Mostly," he said. "You missed a few details, but basically, yes. Yes, Anna was the kid's mother, and Vladimir was the father. And yes, Edgar was the one who arranged the whole thing."

"So what did I miss, Clyde?"

"As I said, a few details. And one important one."

"Such as?"

He said: "Such as, who actually killed the two men. It wasn't me. And there's one more thing I have to tell you."

"What's that?"

"It's about my wife, Daisy. She's pregnant. She was tested, and it's confirmed. We suspected as much, and now it's definite. She's having a baby."

"But I thought...."

"I know what you thought," he said, "but you were wrong." And he got up, quite suddenly, and left the office.

17

I found it impossible to work the rest of the morning. I had to redraft the old lady's will, taking care of her new wishes about the disposal of that stupid strand of pearls. I was also supposed to be working on a minor real estate deal, and another client needed to file for an extension on his income tax return. And still another was about to lease his land for a wind farm. I just couldn't concentrate on any of it. I was too mixed up. Clyde ... it was all so puzzling. I knew I was basically right on one score: little Clyde Jr. was the key to the whole bloody mess. Clyde had admitted it. But there were still some loose ends, some unanswered questions.

And the biggest one of all: who killed those men?

What I didn't realize was how soon I would get the answers. Answers to all the questions I had asked, and more.

I had lunch with a colleague, in my favorite Chinese restaurant. Joe Bailey was a really clever guy, full of high spirits. He collected lawyer jokes, and over a plate of prawns with snowpeas, he regaled me with some prime examples. Then he followed this up with some really juicy gossip about some of my fellow lawyers, especially the romantic adventures of one Judith Regis, who was secretly dating a judge.

And a woman judge at that.

All this was so entertaining, I was able to put the whole affair, the whole business of Vladimir and Edgar and Clyde out of my mind. But when I came back to the office, I was surprised to find Claude Winters waiting for me in the hallway. I motioned him into the office.

"Is this a good time?" he asked. "I need to talk to you."

"Sure thing," I said. "Come right in."

I hadn't seen him very often, and now I looked closely at him, as he sat in a chair across from my desk. It struck me again, how handsome he was, with his shock of dirty blond hair, his blue-green eyes, his well-formed face with its regular features, his lean yet muscular figure. He was wearing chino pants and a plaid shirt. As always, it was striking how little he resembled Clyde physically, and no doubt in other ways as well. He folded his hands in his lap. He seemed brooding, nervous, and somewhat uncomfortable.

"I was talking to my brother," he said. "He told me all about your conversation. And he told you that Daisy was pregnant, right?"

"Yes he did. I was surprised. I had always thought ... well, that she couldn't have children."

"That's what a lot of people think. Or thought. They always do, you know? They blame the woman. But really, it was Clyde all the time. He was the one who couldn't have children. And, like a lot of other things in his life, it was all my fault."

"Your fault?"

"I got sick once, we were kids, and I had a mild case of whatever it was. But Clyde, he caught it from me, and he had a bad case, and, well, this was the result. Not enough sperm, or something like that. They went to all kinds of doctors, but nothing could be done. Daisy—she was half-crazy over the problem, she wanted a child so desperately. They thought about artificial insemination. But Clyde, at first, well, he couldn't stand the idea of Daisy having somebody else's baby. That's why they had to try to adopt. But now things are different. They changed their mind."

"So ... this time, it's artificial insemination? They went to a sperm bank?"

He said. "No, not really."

"I don't understand."

He said: "It's my child. I'm the father. I've been involved with Daisy, practically all my adult life. I've got to tell you about this, because it's relevant. I've done a lot of things in my life that I'm sorry about. You know, we're twins, me and Clyde, but we don't look alike, and we're very different people. We love each other, but we're like night and day. Clyde, he was always serious, a good boy; I was rotten, practically a delinquent. The evil twin, you know? Well, not evil, but … undisciplined. And you know, life just isn't fair. Our mother died when we were teenagers. And that left us with Mose. And Mose loved me. He loved me a lot. Somehow, he never cottoned to Clyde. Clyde was too much of a goody-goody. Me, I was the one he preferred. Maybe he saw his own self in me, the way he had been as a kid, sort of wild and untamed, before he married our mom.

"I got through high school somehow. He sent me to Columbia, which was expensive; God knows how I got in, but I did. I had good board scores. Clyde … well, the family didn't have too much money, so he went to a local college. Willingly. And he worked hard and got good grades, and ended up at Berkeley. Me, I flunked out of Columbia. Too much drinking and drugs and screwing around and sheer laziness. But Mose forgave me for everything. That was true love, I tell you. True love.

"Then I met Daisy. I'd had lots of women. But I really fell for Daisy. Don't ask me why. Love is blind, the way they say it is. It's true. I loved her a lot. And she loved me. But Daisy, she's delicate, she's nervous, and … after a while, she just couldn't take it, I mean, she still loved me, but the way I lived, the way I behaved, and the other women—it wasn't what she wanted, and I don't blame her. She gave me my walking papers. I deserved it. She married Clyde. That was the right thing to do, the smart thing. He was head over heels in love with her, and he didn't care about her connection to me. She never really loved him. And—I'm ashamed to say—she couldn't break off with me, married or not. I just couldn't get her out of my mind, and she felt the same way. And I got her pregnant, too.

"I mean, there's no excuse for that; I shouldn't have been sleeping with my brother's wife, and if I did, I should have been more careful, right? But that's what happened. Clyde didn't know about it, then. She just disappeared, she went away, her plan was, she'd have the baby, give it up for adoption. I don't think she could have gone through with that, but as luck would have it, she miscarried. Still, she told me she didn't want to come back, not to Clyde, she wanted to leave him, and marry me, and we would go off together. But, you know, I just couldn't do it. I'm weak, I'm not a good person, but I just couldn't do that to my brother. I love him, too, maybe more than I love Daisy. And I've ruined his life so many times, I just couldn't break his heart. So I told her no, I couldn't do it. And in the end, she came back, and she and Clyde took up life together again, he never asked questions, and then they adopted little Clyde, and I can't tell you how happy they were. For a while.

"Then came real trouble. That bastard Edgar, it's all his fault. He's the one who arranged the adoption, that worthless shit, and maybe he knew and maybe he didn't know that there was a father somewhere who had never legally given up the kid; mostly he didn't care. Then this Vladimir guy reappeared, and there was hell to pay."

I said: "I told Clyde I thought that's what happened. I guess I got it right."

He said: "Not exactly. You were wrong about two details. One small one and one big one."

"Oh? Which details?"

"The small one was about Vladimir. You think he wanted money. No, he didn't give a shit about money. Edgar and Anna, they wanted money. Vladimir wanted his child. Money we could have given him, maybe. But not the child. That's why he had to be killed."

"And the big mistake?"

"Can't you guess? You thought it was Clyde, you thought Clyde was behind the whole thing, you thought he killed those two guys. But it wasn't Clyde. It was me. I'm the one that got rid of Vladimir. Clyde had nothing to do with it. He didn't even know. And then I did Edgar, too."

I sat there, stunned.

He said, "you're thinking, how could I? How could I take a life? Well, believe me, I didn't want to. But things in this world aren't as simple as we might want them to be. It was ... maybe a life for a life. If Daisy lost the child, I don't think she could go on living. I really mean it. She's that fragile, and the kid means so much to her. And then, if she couldn't live, well, that would ruin Clyde's life, too; he'd lose his kid, and he'd lose her too. I felt, I had to do it. I just had to. I hoped they wouldn't catch me, but if they did, I was prepared to pay the price. I owed it to them."

I couldn't get a word out. I just sat there, in shock.

He went on: "For a while, I *was* paying a price—in money that is. I paid Edgar, I paid Anna. I had an inheritance from my mother, and that's where it went. That's all *they* wanted; the greedy pigs, they were just after the money. I don't know how long it could have gone on, but anyway, so far, it was just money. But when Vladimir came—you have to understand, he didn't know about the kid, not at first. He and Anna had split up, and he'd gone back to Russia. He didn't know she was pregnant; then he got a letter from her, in Russia, she said she was pregnant, but she said, she didn't want the kid, she was going to get an abortion. Maybe she really intended to do that. Then Edgar stepped in. He told Anna she could make big money, just have the child and give it up, he knew somebody who would pay a lot of money for a child. She jumped at the chance. Edgar told Clyde, he could get them a kid, just the kind they wanted, a newborn American kid, they wouldn't have to go to China or Bolivia or whatever; they'd have to pay, but it was perfectly legal. And they jumped at the chance. They were willing to pay anything. And Edgar kept assuring them, it was all strictly kosher, which of course wasn't true. But how were they to know? I mean, it was all done in court, it was a legal adoption—well, it seemed that way. Nobody was talking about Vladimir. In fairness to Edgar, he never expected Vladimir to show up. But he did.

"Anna ... she knew that Vladimir would never agree to give up the baby, but she figured, nobody had to know, and he was in Russia, anyway. So she wrote him a letter and said, she had an abortion, that's the end of it. But Vladimir, he knew her too well; he never trusted her, and he smelled a rat. He wrote and asked, where did you get the abortion, who did it, how much did it cost, and Anna gave him fishy answers.

"Anyway, to make a long story short, he came back to this country, and he snooped around, and he found out, there was no abortion, she had given birth.... Meanwhile, she had moved around, this place and that place, and it was hard to trace her; but then she came back here, and he got wind of it, and also that the kid had been adopted. She had reconnected with Edgar, and they were doing stuff together. Edgar was desperate for money, and they were planning to get money, by stealing it from Zack. And they decided, too, to get Anna pregnant again, never mind from whom, and sell this baby to Clyde and Daisy, or, if they didn't want it, to somebody else. Edgar knew there was a market. Anyway, that was what those two were planning to do....

"So now Vladimir was on the scene, and he found out what had happened; he knew about Edgar, and the adoption, and so he went to Edgar, and he demanded his child back. He said he was the father, and he never gave up his rights, which was true, of course; and they tried stalling him, trying to talk him out of it, I don't know exactly how. Meanwhile, they see more of a chance to make money: they can demand more cash, they can threaten Clyde and Daisy with Vladimir. And Vladimir, he's playing his own game, he gets in touch with Clyde, tells him the kid is his, that he never gave up his rights, and he's going to go to court if necessary, to get his child. Clyde is horrified, of course; he tries to keep it from Daisy, he tries to offer money, he vows to fight it out.... He told me everything, he told me, too, that he didn't know what to do, he went to Edgar, and Edgar finally told him the truth, that the adoption very likely wasn't valid, a father has rights, and Vladimir never signed anything, and Edgar wants more money, he makes a lame excuse, he'll fix everything up, he'll pay Vladimir off. Clyde also decides to try to deal with Vladimir. But Vladimir refuses, he wants the child, nothing else, no money, nothing, just the child. Still, they keep talking, and he agrees to meet Clyde, but in secret, without telling Edgar; and they make a date, for Lytton Park. Of course Clyde tells me all about it, we don't have secrets from each other. And it's going to be a late night meeting, after Daisy and the rest of the house are asleep. So I arrange to meet Vladimir first, I gave him some excuse, I said I had a proposition , maybe we could make a deal; and I went there ahead of Clyde, and I did what I had to do."

"You had Zack's gun...."

"I did. I knew he had a gun, and I just went there one day, I went to talk to Anna, and while I was there, I took it. Look: I didn't want to kill Vladimir, he never did me any harm; I know it was wrong. But it was him or my family, and I couldn't let that happen. I threatened him, he thought I was bluffing, he said he would never give up his son. So I shot him. I figured, once he was dead, he had no more rights, OK? That was the end of the custody business. But there was still Edgar to deal with, and Anna."

"Edgar ... but why? You had to get rid of Vladimir, he was the father. But why Edgar?"

"He was squeezing us for money, that was bad enough. But even though Vladimir was dead—Edgar didn't know who did it, naturally; I think he suspected Clyde. And then he told Clyde, don't think you're out of the woods. He said, remember, I arranged the adoption, and I could go to the judge, and tell him, the whole thing was a fraud, the adoption was illegal, there was a father, and he never relinquished his rights, so, even though he's dead, you can set the adoption aside. And then Anna will get back her baby."

"She actually wanted the child?"

"No, no way. She couldn't have cared less. Edgar just said she did. He was, as usual, a goddamn liar. But I couldn't take the chance. Edgar was serious about some things. Money, actually. He was desperate for money. Even if he was fooling, he would never stop squeezing us for money. So I saw, I had to finish the job. I went to the house, and I did what I had to do. Again. When I was done, I took the gun one day, and I put it back in Zack's drawer."

"And Anna?"

"I warned her. Get out of town. I went to the house, and took the gun out of the drawer again. I showed it to her. She said, where did you get that? I said, out of the drawer in this very house. So she knew I was telling the truth. And I told her, I'm not afraid to use it. She said, I'm pregnant.... I asked her, who's the father. She said, maybe Martin Greenhouse, maybe some other guy. She blamed it all on Edgar, it was strictly a financial proposition, she said, I don't really want the baby. And I said, you've made enough trouble. We don't want this brat. If you know what's good for you, you'll get the hell out of here. Go back to Russia, or wherever. I waved the gun in her face. And if you ever squawk, to the police, or anybody, I'll find a way to get you. She believed me. And so she went; she got out of there and fast."

"Why did you put the gun back in the drawer? That seems stupid."

"It was worse than stupid. Zack saw me, but that didn't matter. He has no short-term memory, he's getting worse. I should have thrown the gun away, in a dumpster, or tossed it into the Bay, but I thought nobody would ever think to connect it with these murders; and if they did, so what? They'd think it was Anna."

"And what about Melissa?"

"Same thing as Anna. I told her it would be best for her health if she got the hell out of here. She took the hint."

"You told them you killed Edgar?"

"Not in so many words. But they got the point."

"Does ... Clyde know this? About you? What you did?"

He paused for a second. "He does now. I think he suspected before. About Vladimir. You know, when he got there, in Lytton Park, Vladimir was dead. It could have been some mugger, but ... Clyde after all had told me he was meeting Vladimir in Lytton Park. So he had to have had a pretty damn good idea. But he never said anything. Even when the police started breathing down his neck. Clyde isn't that kind of a guy. He would never betray me. But I couldn't let this go on. I told him everything. And I'm going to give the whole story to the police. I'll tell them every last detail. And I'll even give them proof, if they need proof."

"And ... you're willing ... to go to prison?"

"Willing to go to prison? No. Look, I'm only human. Who

wants to rot in a cell for the rest of their life? If I have to go, I'll go. But first, I'm going to try to get away, leave the country, go someplace, I don't know, India, Brazil, who knows where. I'll start a new life. If it doesn't work, or if they catch me, well, that's the breaks."

"And Daisy?"

"She's got my baby inside of her. Clyde knows that too. He's my brother. He's forgiven me for everything. He knows I did a lot of bad things, like what I did with Daisy. And killing two people—that's something so far beyond anything Clyde could have done; and it's hard for him to understand. But he knows I love him, and I did it for him, and for Daisy. Now I'm getting out of their lives. I'm leaving them a baby. It's going to be raised as Clyde's baby. It'll never know the truth. That's the way it's going to be. I want it that way. I'll be the bad uncle, the missing uncle, the uncle who killed somebody and ran away; or the uncle in prison, whatever.... I don't really care one way or the other. I'll *know* it's my kid, and I'll follow it, as it grows up, I'll find a way to get in touch with Clyde. This sounds crazy, but I'm sure it's a boy. I want a son. I've always wanted a son. The first time Daisy was pregnant, it was a boy. And I'd like little Clyde to have a baby brother. And I think big Clyde, too, he'd love to have another son.

"As I told you, I really hope I can get away with it. I think I can. I've got a little bit of money, I've got an airline ticket and a passport. And I don't really feel truly guilty. I don't want to go to jail. But, you know, if it happens, it happens. I did the right thing. I cleaned the slate."

"But ... why are you telling me this? Aren't you afraid I'll go to the police?"

"You won't need to. They'll know the whole story, soon enough. I've written it out, a full confession. They'll get it and they'll know I'm telling the truth. But by that time, I'll be gone. And I'm telling you because—because you talked to Clyde, and because you guessed part of it, and decided he was the one, the one who did it. So I had this feeling, I had to come talk to you, straighten you out. I didn't want you to do anything foolish. And I thought maybe, just maybe, you'd understand."

I sat there speechless. I looked at him closely. He had talked calmly, coherently, but I could see the agitation, the despair, behind the words. I felt somehow paralyzed by all the things he had revealed. Maybe he was waiting for some sort of reaction on my part. But I couldn't pull myself together and say anything to Claude. It was just too much for me.

He could see my embarrassment. He could see how hard it was to digest all the things he had said. He started to say something more, stopped, thought better of it, then added, "Well, that's it; I'll just say goodbye. Wish me good luck."

I said nothing. I'm sorry to this day that I kept silent, but I had no choice. I couldn't get a word out to save my life. And Claude got up, and left my office.

18

I never saw Claude Winters again. I don't really know what happened to him. I suspect he got away, and started some sort of life in another country. I'm not sure if the family stayed in touch with him. I never connected with the rest of them either. Too bad, because I lost them as clients. I don't think it was because of any work I did, I think they just found the whole episode too painful, and they too wanted to start over.

I did get an announcement of the birth of Daisy's child. Claude had been wrong. It was not a boy. It was a little girl, seven pounds, three ounces. The announcement named the parents as Clyde and Daisy Winters. The baby's name was Claudia.

A friend of the family told me once, rather casually, that Mose, despite his age and fragility, had gone away on a long, mysterious trip, and told nobody where he was going. Maybe he was just getting in a Caribbean cruise, or touring the Greek Islands, while he still had the strength. But more likely he was visiting his wayward son, the son he had always loved—loved too much probably—the son he surely missed so badly. I wondered, too, whether he ever finished the book he told me he was writing. I doubt it. As far as I know, it hasn't been published; and he's never been interviewed by Oprah or anybody else on TV. There's never been this program featuring old Thutmose Winters, the octogenarian author of a sensational book. I think that book will never be finished, and will never see the light of day. It doesn't matter.

* * *

A year or two after these events, Uncle Zack died, after what was described in the obituary as a "long illness." I found out later that the end was quite peaceful and that Zack's last year had been reasonably happy. He had become, in the end, quite fond of the Tongan woman. He loved it when she gave him a bath. He even asked her to marry him. Fortunately, she already had a husband—another Tongan, who matched her in size and in shape. This guy, I was told, worked in a car wash. In his spare time, they say, he was an amateur sumo wrestler.

Anyway, Zack had slowly declined, and eventually "joined the majority," as somebody once put it, that is, the billions and billions who have come and gone on this earth. Sad but true. Right now, I'm glad to be part of the living minority.

I read the news of Zack's death in the local paper, and I decided, on the spur of the moment, to go to the funeral. I was hoping the family might yet relent, and hire me to handle the estate. I knew it was not very large, as estates go; but I don't throw any business away. I also knew that getting it was a long, long, long shot. Probably I was the last person they would ever think of hiring, at this stage of the game. Still, I had nothing to lose but an hour or two of my time.

As I expected, my suspicions were correct; I was wasting my time.

There were not many people at the funeral. A few old-timers tottered in with their canes and their walkers. The woman from Tonga showed up, with her husband. Mose wasn't there. I suppose he was, by then, too old and frail. I did see Clyde and Daisy, with their two children in tow. Clyde Jr. seemed to remember me, because he rushed up and kicked me in the shins. Clyde nodded to me, but seemed distant and embarrassed. Cynthia, who was with them, behaved much the same. They obviously didn't feel like talking to me. Claude's behavior was, I suppose, something of an open wound. Maybe, in some crazy way, they associated all this sadness and heartache with me.

They had been good clients, and I regretted losing them. Oh well, life goes on. Fortunately, I have other clients, good clients; people who have personal and financial troubles—which means legal troubles too. Good clients: clients who never get mixed up in murder, and who never drag me down into that kind of mess, kicking and screaming all the way. Those are the clients I prefer.

* * *

About the author

Lawrence Friedman is a professor of law at Stanford University. He teaches courses in American legal history and law and society. He is the author of *A History of American Law*, *Crime and Punishment in American History*, *The Human Rights Culture*, and *Total Justice*, among other works.

In 2015 Friedman published *The Big Trial: Law as Public Spectacle*, which vividly recounts famous cases in history and their media coverage of the day. He also recently published *Dead Hands: A Social History of Wills, Trusts, and Inheritances*, a subject which is the backbone of Frank May's (fictional) practice.

Visit us at *www.qpbooks.com.*

www.ingramcontent.com/pod-product-compliance
Lightning Source LLC
Chambersburg PA
CBHW071211260626
47162CB00004B/1253